A Time to Turn

A Time to Turn

Anglican Readings for Lent and Easter Week

Compiled by
Christopher L. Webber

MOREHOUSE PUBLISHING
A Continuum imprint
HARRISBURG • LONDON • NEW YORK

Morehouse Publishing, P.O. Box 1321, Harrisburg, PA 17105

Morehouse Publishing, The Tower Building, 11 York Road, London SE1 7NX

Morehouse Publishing is a Continuum imprint.

Excerpt from *Christus Veritas* by William Temple. Copyright © by William Temple. Used by permission from Macmillan, London, UK.

Excerpt from *A Ray of Darkness* by Rowan Williams. Copyright 1995 by Rowan Williams. Used by permission from Cowley Publications, Cambridge, Massachusetts.

Excerpt from *Open to Judgment* by Rowan Williams. Copyright © 1994 by Rowan Williams. Used by permission from Darton, Longman, and Todd, London, UK.

Cover art: *Temptations of Jesus*, courtesy of The Crosiers

Cover design by Laurie Klein Westhafer

Library of Congress Cataloging-in-Publication Data

A time to turn : Anglican readings for Lent and Easter week / compiled by Christopher L. Webber.
    p. cm.
Includes bibliographical references.
    ISBN 0-8192-2110-4 (pbk.)
    1. Lent—Prayer-books and devotions—English. 2. Holy Week—Prayer-books and devotions—English. 3. Anglican Communion—Prayer-books and devotions—English. I. Webber, Christopher.
    BV85.A15 2004
    242'.34—dc22
                                2004007004

Printed in the United States of America

04 05 06 07 08 09   10 9 8 7 6 5 4 3 2 1

Contents

Introduction

Time constantly turns; winter comes after fall, and then spring and then summer, season after season in a perpetual round. We human beings are caught up in that turning, not only season after season but week after week. Our lives repeat themselves; we dread Mondays and look forward to Fridays. Patterns have value, of course; it simplifies our lives if we can do again what we have done before.

Nonetheless, the Bible speaks again and again of broken patterns. God says through the prophet, "I am doing a new thing. Do you not see it?" There is value in routine, but God calls on us sometimes to turn in a new direction, to turn away from the familiar routine of death and seek life, real life.

Lent is above all a time of turning. Lent provides us with a time in which we can break away from the old, familiar, and deadly patterns we so easily fall into and open ourselves to the possibility of something new. Lent is a time to turn.

When we turn away from the compulsions and distractions of our daily lives and seek a new direction, we may discover—to our surprise—that our world has also begun to move toward patterns of life that have much in common with the ancient disciplines of the Christian Church. The Church has recommended prayer, fasting, and charity. The need for these is evident now on every side and interest in them is growing—though often by other names and in places other than churches.

In a world of pressures and distractions, the world is rediscovering the value of contemplation and of exploring the spiritual side of our nature. In a world where some are overweight and many are hungry, the rich world debates the virtues of various diet plans. In a world where some are rich and many are poor, appeals for donations come at us from every side.

No wonder the church has always commended prayer and fasting and charity. What, then, can we learn from those who were more familiar with these practices? How can we use the season of Lent to rediscover them for ourselves?

Anglicans are fortunate to have a tradition nearly five centuries old that has used the same language we speak today and needs little editing to speak with force and clarity to us. There are numerous men and women from whom we can still learn. Names like Thomas Cranmer, John Donne, and Harriet Beecher Stowe are well known. Others, such as Elizabeth Rowe, Mark Frank, William Law, and Myles Coverdale, are less well known but deserve a wider audience.

These readings are arranged in a regular sequence through each week. Ash Wednesday and the days before the first Sunday in Lent bring us some general considerations on the meaning of the season. The next five weeks all follow the same pattern. Sundays, not technically a part of Lent, are used to meditate on God's love; Mondays focus on the need for discipline; Tuesdays on fasting; Wednesdays on prayer; Thursdays on charity. Friday prepares us for Good Friday in Holy Week by providing readings on the cross. Finally, because Lent was first of all the season in which new converts prepared themselves for baptism, the Saturday readings ask us to remember our own baptism and the new life that began in us at the font and that needs always to be renewed and nurtured. In Holy Week, the pattern is changed and the readings focus directly on the meaning of Christ's death. Finally, Easter and the days of Easter week provide meditations on the meaning of the resurrection.

Each reading is followed by a brief phrase from the passage for that day to be used as a focus for thought during the day and a way to remember and ponder on what we have read. It would be useful to read these passages in the context of prayer and to spend some time in silence immediately after the reading to allow the words to sink more deeply into our minds and souls.

Because these passages are intended for use by twenty-first-century Christians who may not be professional scholars and who do not ordinarily encounter the cadences of Elizabethan English in their reading,

I have modernized spellings and phrases wherever I thought it would be helpful. For the same reason, most scriptural quotations have been conformed to the New Revised Standard Version of the Bible.

The library staffs at St. Mark's Library of the General Theological Seminary, the Watkinson Library at Trinity College Hartford, the Olin Library at Wesleyan University in Middletown, and the Beinecke Library at Yale University in New Haven have been unfailingly helpful to me in compiling this material and I am grateful to them.

Brief biographies of the authors are provided at the end of the book. There is also a bibliography for those who might like to become better acquainted with these great teachers of our past and make them friends and guides for the present.

The Ash Wednesday Collect
(Paraphrased)

Almighty God of everlasting years,

Who in your love and mercy cannot hate

What you have made, and who, when we with tears

And contrite hearts repent, forgives; Create

And make in us hearts penitent and new,

That we, lamenting worthily our sin,

May find, O God most merciful, in you

Forgiveness, and a better life begin.

–Christopher L. Webber

Ash Wednesday

A reading from a sermon by Lancelot Andrewes preached before King James I on Ash Wednesday, 1619, on the text: "Yet even now, says the LORD, return to me with all your heart, with fasting, with weeping, and with mourning; rend your hearts and not your clothing. Return to the LORD, your God" (Joel 2:12–13).

For this time the Church has chosen this text. This is the time in which, however we have dispensed with it all the rest of the year, she would have us seriously to intend and make it our time of turning to the Lord; for she holds it unsafe to leave us wholly to ourselves, to take any time, it matters not when, lest we take none at all.

And the reason is that once a year all things turn. And that once is now, at this time, for now at this time is the turning of the year. In heaven the sun is at the equinox; the zodiac and all the constellations in it, do now turn about to their first point. The earth and all her plants, after a dead winter, return to the first and best season of the year. The creatures, the fowls of the air, the swallow and the turtledove, the crane and the stork, know their seasons and make their just return at this time every year. Everything now turning, we also should make it our time in which to turn to God.

Then, because this day is known as the first day of Lent, it fits well as a welcome into this time, a time lent us, as it were, by God, set us by the Church, in which to make our turning.

Repentance itself is nothing else but a kind of circling: to turn to the One by repentance from whom, by sin, we have turned away.

First, then, there is a turn in which we look forward to God and with our whole heart resolve to turn to God. Then there is a turn again in which we look backward to our sins in which we have turned from God; and with beholding them our very heart must break. There is one turn resolving to amend that which is to come; another reflecting and sorrowing for that which is past; one turn declining from evil to be done hereafter, another sentencing itself for evil done before.

To turn is a counsel given to those who are out of the right way, for going on still and turning are opposite motions, both of them with reference to a way. If the way is good, we are to hold on; if otherwise, to turn and take another.

From God then, as from the journey's end of our life, our way, we are never to turn our steps or our eyes, but still to walk with God all our life long.

When any danger of death is near, indeed if we but sadly think about it, a certain chilliness takes us and we cannot with any comfort think of our journey's end. We hear a voice crying behind us, "That is not the way; this that you have lost is your way: walk in it." That voice, if we hear it not, is a result of the noise around us. If we would sometimes go aside into some retired place, or in the still of the night listen to it, we might by some chance hear it.

To be turned, I call, when by some cross of body or mind (as it were with a ring in our nose), we are brought around, whether we will it or not, to see how we have gone astray.

To be turned, I call, when the world ministers to us no cause of heaviness; yet even then, the grace of God moving us, we set ourselves around and holding those former conversions before us we work it out, having no heavy impulse from outside to force us to it. The one who is under no arrest, with no bridle in the jaw, who shall in the time of peace resolve on a time for turning and take it: that person has great cause to rejoice, and to rejoice before God.

Walk with God all our life long.

Thursday after Ash Wednesday

A reading on sin from a sermon by John Donne on the text, "For my iniquities overwhelm me; like a heavy burden they are too much for me to bear" (Psalm 38:4).

I cannot excuse my sins because of the example of my father, nor can I excuse them because of the times, or because of the ill disposition that rules society now, and do ill because everybody else does so. To say there is a rot, therefore the sheep must perish, corruptions in religion have crept in and work in every corner, and therefore God's sheep, simple souls, must be content to admit the infection of this rot; that there is a murrain, and therefore cattle must die; superstition practiced in many places, and therefore the strong servants of God must come to sacrifice their obedience to it, or their blood for it. There is no such rot, no such murrain, no such corruption of the times as can lay a necessity, or can afford an excuse to those who are corrupted with the times. It is not such a peace as takes away honor that secures a nation, nor such a peace as takes away zeal that secures a conscience, so neither is it an observation of what others do or are inclined to do but what truth and integrity you decline from that needs to be considered.

It is not the sin of your father, not the sin of the times, not the sin of your own years, that you should say in your old age, in excuse of your covetousness, I have lived temperately, continently, all my life and therefore may be allowed one sin for my ease in my old age. Or that you should say in your youth, I will retire in my old age and live contentedly then with a little, but now, how vain it would be to attempt to keep out the tide or quench the heat and impetuous violence of youth. For if you think it enough to say, I have only lived as others have lived, you will find some examples to die by also, and die as other old men and women, old in years and old in sins, have died also: negligently or fearfully, without any sense at all, or all their sense turned into fearful apprehension and desperation.

They are not such sins as those of that age need to commit, nor such sins as those of your calling or your profession cannot avoid; so that you should say, I shall not be believed to understand my profession, as well as others, if I do not live by it as well as others do. Is there no way to be a carpenter, except that after he has been made warm by the chips, and baked, and roasted by it, it is necessary to make an idol of the wood, and worship? Is there no way to be a silversmith, without needing to make shrines for Diana of the Ephesians as Demetrius did? No way to be a lawyer without serving the passion of the client? No way to be a preacher without sowing pillows under great men's elbows? It is not the sin of your calling that oppresses you. God has instituted callings for the conservation of order in general, not for the justification of disorders in any particular. For those who justify their faults by their calling, have not yet received that calling from above, which is where they must be justified and sanctified on the way and glorified in the end. There is no lawful calling in which you may not be honest.

You cannot excuse yourself by the unjust command of your superior; nor the ill example of your pastor, whose life counter-preaches his doctrine, for that shall aggravate his, but not excuse your sin; nor the influence of stars, or such a working of a necessary and inevitable and unconditioned decree of God as may obstruct a religious walking in this life, or a happy resting in the life to come. It is none of these, not the sin of your Father, not the sin of the present times, not the sin of your years and age nor of your calling, nor of the magistrate, nor of your pastor, nor of destiny, nor of decrees, but it is your sin, your own sin.

It is your sin.

Friday after Ash Wednesday

A reading on sin from a sermon by Jeremy Taylor on
"The Christian Conquest over the Body of Sin," based on
the text, "For I do not do the good I want, but the evil I
do not want is what I do" (Romans 7:19).

The law of God without is opposed by a law of sin within. We
have a corrupted nature, and a body of infirmity, and our
reason dwells in the dark, and we must go out of the world
before we leave our sin. Justice is too often taught to bow to great
interests, we cannot live without flattery; and there are some trades
that minister to sin, so that without a sin we cannot maintain our
families; and if you mean to live, you must do as others do. Now so
long as people see that they are likely to be undone by innocence, and
that they cannot live except by compliance with the evil customs of
the world, they must conclude that because they must live, they must
sin; they must live handsomely, and, therefore, must do some things
unhandsomely; and so sin is unavoidable.

We have brought ourselves into an accidental necessity of sinning,
by the evil principles which are sucked in by great parts of mankind.
We are taught ways of going to heaven without forsaking our sins; of
repentance without restitution; of being in charity without hearty
forgiveness and without love; of believing our sins to be pardoned
before they are mortified; of trusting in Christ's death without conformity to his life; of being in God's favor only on account of being of
such an opinion.

To our weak and corrupted nature and our foolish discourses, we
daily add on evil habits and customs of sinning. "An evil custom is a
hook in the soul," said one of the Patristic teachers, "and draws it

whither the devil pleases." When it comes to St. Peter's word concerning "hearts trained in greed," then it is also "weak," and unable to do the good it wishes to do, or to avoid the evil which it pretends to hate. This is so known, I shall not insist on it; but add this only: that wherever a habit is contracted, it is all one what the instance be; it is easy as delicious, as unalterable in virtue as in vice; for what helps nature bring to a vicious habit, the same and much more the Spirit of God, by power and by comforts, can do in a virtuous; and then we are well again. You see by this who are, and why they are, in this evil condition. The evil natures, and the evil principles, and the evil manners of the world, these are the causes of our imperfect willings and weaker actings in the things of God; and as long as we stay here, sin will be unavoidable.

If this is true, God will be poorly served. If it is not true, most of us will have small hope of being saved, because this is the condition of most people. Now if this is a state of regeneration, I wonder what is, or can be, a state of reprobation, for though this is the state of nature, yet it cannot be the state of one redeemed by the Spirit of Christ; and, therefore, do not flatter yourselves any more, that it is enough for you to have good desires and bad performances: never think that any sin can reign in you, and yet you can be servants of God; that sin can dwell in you, and at the same time the Spirit of God can dwell in you too; or that life and death can abide together. The sum of affairs is this: "If you live according to the flesh, you will die; but if by the Spirit you put to death the deeds of the body, you will live."

Life and death cannot abide together.

Saturday after Ash Wednesday

A reading on sin from a sermon by Jeremy Taylor on "The Christian Conquest over the Body of Sin," based on the text, "For I do not do the good I want, but the evil I do not want is what I do" (Romans 7:19).

What then? Cannot sin be avoided? Cannot a Christian mortify the deeds of the body? Cannot Christ redeem us, and cleanse us from all our sins? Cannot the works of the devil be destroyed? That is the question to be asked: Whether or not it is necessary, and therefore very possible, for a servant of God to pass from this evil state of things, and not only hate evil but avoid it also?

Some cannot choose but sin; "for the carnal mind is not subject to God, neither indeed can be," says St. Paul; but there are also some who cannot endure anything that is not good. It is a great pain for a temperate man to suffer the disorders of drunkenness, and the shames of lust are intolerable to a chaste and modest person. This also is affirmed by St. John: "Those who have been born of God do not sin." So you see it is possible for a good person not to commit the sin to which we may be tempted. But the apostle says more: "They cannot sin, because they have been born of God."

And this is agreeable to the words of our blessed Savior: "A good tree cannot bear bad fruit, nor can a bad tree bear good fruit." That is, as the child of hell does not check at sin, but does it, and is not troubled; so, on the other side, a child of God is as fully convinced of righteousness; and that which is unrighteous is as hateful to him as colocynths to the taste, or the sharpest punctures to the pupil of the eye. We may see something of this in common experience. What person of ordinary prudence and reputation can be tempted to steal? or, for what price would that person be tempted to murder a friend? Does not every good person overcome all the power of great sins? Can we, by the Spirit of God and right reason, by fear and hope, conquer the giant Goliath, and yet not overcome the little children of Gath? Is it harder to overcome a little sin than a great one? Are not the temptations to little sins very little? Are they greater and stronger than a mighty grace? "I can do all things through him who strengthens me," says St. Paul; "If God is for us, who is against us?. . . No, in all these things we are more than conquerors." For even among an army of conquerors there are degrees of exaltation: some serve God like the centurion, and some like St. Peter; some like Martha, and some like Mary: all good people conquer their temptation, but some with more ease, and some with a clearer victory.

To sum up all: every good person is a new creature, and Christianity is not so much a divine institution, as a divine frame and temper of spirit; which if we heartily pray for, and endeavor to obtain, we shall find it as hard and as uneasy to sin against God, as now we think it impossible to abstain from our most pleasing sins. For the Holy Spirit of God, and the word of God, and the grace of God changes dullness into zeal, and fear into love, and sinful habits into innocence, and passes on from grace to grace, till we arrive at the full measure of the stature of Christ, and into the perfect liberty of the children of God; so that we shall hate what God hates; and the evil that is forbidden, we shall not do; not because we are strong of ourselves, but because Christ is our strength, and he is in us; and Christ's strength shall be perfected in our weakness, and his grace will be sufficient for us; and he will of his own good pleasure work in us, not only to will, but also to do, says the apostle, "to will and to work for his good pleasure" and fully, being sanctified throughout, to the glory of his holy name, and the eternal salvation of our souls, through Jesus Christ.

Christ's grace will be sufficient for us.

The First Week of Lent

Lent

Welcome dear feast of Lent: who loves you not,
Authority and temperance as well loves not
    But is composed of passion.
The Scriptures bid us fast, the Church says Now;
Give to your Mother what you would allow
    To every Corporation.

The humble soul, composed of love and fear,
Begins at home and lays the burden there
    When doctrines disagree
And says, In things which custom rightly got,
I am a scandal to the Church, and not
    The Church is so to me.

It's true we cannot reach Christ's fortieth day,
Yet to go part of that religious way
    Is better than to rest;
We cannot match our Savior's purity
Yet are we told: Be holy even as he.
    In both, let's do our best.

One going in the way that Christ has gone
Is much more sure to meet with him than one
    Who travels by-ways.
Perhaps my God, although so far before,
May turn and take me by the hand, and more
    May strengthen my decays.

Yet, Lord, instruct us to improve our fast
By starving sin and taking such repast
    As may our faults control,
That each of us may revel at the door,
Not in the parlor, banqueting the poor
    And among those my soul.

–George Herbert

The First Sunday in Lent

A reading from a meditation on God's love by Elizabeth Rowe.

O Lord God, permit a worthless creature to plead a little with you. What honor will my destruction bring you? what profit, what triumph to the Almighty will my perdition be? Mercy is your brightest attribute; this gives you all your loveliness, and completes your beauty. By names of kindness and indulgence you have chosen to reveal yourself to us, by titles of the most tender meaning you have made yourself known to my soul: titles which you do not yet disdain, but are still compassionate, and ready to pardon.

But that you have or will forgive me, O my God, aggravates my guilt. And will you indeed forgive me? will you remit the gloomy score, and restore the privilege I have forfeited? Wondrous love! astonishing benignity! let me never live to repeat my ingratitude; let me never live to break my penitent vows; let me die before that unhappy moment arrives.

Almighty Love, the theme of every heavenly song! infinite Grace, the wonder of angels! forgive a mortal tongue that attempts thy praise; and yet should we be silent, the mute creation would find a voice to upbraid us.

But, oh, in what language shall I speak? with what circumstance shall I begin? Shall I roll back the volumes of eternity, and begin with the glorious design that determined our redemption before the birth of Time, before the confines of Creation were fixed?

Infinite years before the day,
Or heavens began to roll?

Shall I speak in general of all the nations of the redeemed? or to excite my own gratitude, shall I consider myself, my worthless self, included, by an eternal decree, among the number of those who should hear of a Redeemer's name and be marked out a partaker of that immense privilege? Before the foundations of the hills were laid the gracious design was formed, and the blessed plan of it schemed out before the curtains of the sky were spread.

Lord! what are we? what am I? what is all the human race, to be so regarded? O narrow thoughts, and narrower words! here confess your defects. These are heights not to be reached by you. Adorable measures of infinite clemency! unsearchable riches of grace! with what astonishment do I survey you! I am swallowed and lost in the glorious immensity. All hail, you divine mysteries! you glorious paths of the unsearchable Deity: let me adore though I can never express you.

Yet should I be silent, heaven and earth, no, hell itself, would reproach me; the damned themselves would call me ungrateful, should I fail to celebrate that grace, whose loss they are for ever lamenting, a loss that leaves them for ever desperate and undone. 'Tis this grace which tunes the harps of heaven, and yields them an immortal subject of harmony and praise. The spirits of just men made perfect fix their contemplations here; they adore the glorious mystery, and while they sing the wonders of redeeming love, they subscribe sublime and living honors to the one who sits on the throne and to the Lamb for ever. And infinitely worthy are you, O Lord, to receive the grateful homage. Who shall not praise and magnify your name? who shall deny the tribute of your glory?

But alas! what can mortals add to you? what can nothingness and vanity give? We murmur from the dust, and attempt your praise from the depths of misery. Yet you condescend to hear and listen to our broken accents; amid the hallelujahs of angels our groans ascend to you, our complaints reach you; from the height of your happiness and from the exaltations of eternal glory, you have a regard to us, poor wretched humanity! You receive our homage with delight, our praises mingle with the harmony of angels, nor interrupt the sacred concord. Those natives of heaven whose morning stars sing together in their heavenly beatitudes, nor disdain to let the children of earth and mortality join with them in celebrating the honors of Jesus, their Lord and ours. To him be every tongue devoted, and let every creature for ever praise God. Amen.

Who shall not praise God?

Monday in the First Week of Lent

A reading on the value of discipline from a sermon by
Richard Meux Benson on the theme of redemption.

Strange and incomprehensible to the world is the life of the
Christian, because we are strangers and pilgrims in the midst
of the world. The world cannot conceive of that on which its
whole being rests, as if it were all darkness. It is ready enough to accept
certain regulations for its outer guidance derived from the revelation
of God. The moral sense of the natural heart acknowledges the truth
of large portions of the divine message. Only it will not surrender the
substantial value of the present course of things. While here it would
seek to be at home here, even though forced to confess that that home
cannot last for long. It has no eye to the heavenly life, and cannot
understand how the affections are to take root in the invisible.

No wonder surely! This world bears many a token of its heavenly
architect. It is no wonder that it fills the heart with joy. Alas, that it should
so occupy the heart of any as to exclude the supreme devotion and love
which belongs to the Creator of all! "Those who are unspiritual do not
receive the gifts of God's Spirit, for they are foolishness to them, and they
are unable to understand them because they are spiritually discerned."

O my friends, labor here on earth that you may attain the home
where the light of the Lamb is ever shining. As the heart of the Son of
God has embraced you in its redeeming love, live in that love,
although to the world it is incomprehensible. Stronger than the world
is that love. That love is the beginning of your redemption, the
strength of your life, the consummation of your sanctity. It is an ample
recompense for the toils and isolation of a pilgrim-life, to know that
we have a place in the heart of Jesus. Let your outer life be evermore

in correspondence with the movement of that heart of surpassing sanctity. Take not your law of action from the dictates of the world, even under its fairest phase. What store shall we set upon the judgment of the world when we are called to enter into the opened gates of that blest home? We shall indeed be happy if all our efforts have been directed towards that great end. Every shorter aim will be found to have failed us. Every bold aspiration of divine faith will be found to be abundantly compensated in the embrace of the eternal love of him who has called us to himself.

Let us not think, my friends, that we can have our home there, unless we have our warfare here. It is the condition of our present existence, that there must ever be a warfare against the soul. This was the second point for our consideration.

It seems to many as if there were no such necessary antagonism between flesh and spirit, the life of earth and the life of heaven. Oh! that is because they know Christianity only as an earthly system, and know not Christ as the Redeemer in whom alone life is to be found. An outer discipline may bring some of the bodily passion under control. Yet will the lusts of the flesh be ever hindering the progress of the spiritual faculties towards the apprehension of Christ in his glory. For this we must rise *out of* ourselves. The innocent gratifications of self—innocent, as some may call them—nevertheless hold down the faculties from that higher aim. It is in the subjugation of our own created nature, with its proud and earthly will, that we rise upward to the life renewed in holiness after the image of the one who created us. O ceaseless battle! How is it to be fought? What vantage-ground have we on which to take our post while wrestling thus with our own selves? Our feet must rest firmly on the Rock of Ages. In the person of our risen Savior we must find a second self, a new life. In that personality we must find a power equal to coping with our miserable personality, which still gathers round itself the vestiges of the old nature tainted with sin. Identified with Christ, we can struggle against ourselves. Not in any other way. Christ has ransomed us from the world. Our individuality is itself a part of that worldly system from which we are redeemed. We are redeemed in Christ from things around us. We are redeemed in Christ from our own selves.

We are strangers and pilgrims in the world.

Tuesday in the First Week of Lent

A reading from a sermon on fasting by Francis E. Paget
on the text: "And whenever you fast, do not look dismal,
like the hypocrites, for they disfigure their faces so as to
show others that they are fasting. Truly I tell you, they
have received their reward. But when you fast, put oil on
your head and wash your face, so that your fasting may
be seen not by others but by your Father who is in secret;
and your Father who sees in secret will reward you"
(Matthew 6:16–18).

It is no argument against fasting to say that the custom has
grown obsolete, and that few now-a-days practice it; because in
the first place, no earnest-minded Christian will ever think of
taking the habits of the world as a rule of action: and secondly, those
who fast according to the directions given by our blessed Lord, will
fast in such a secret manner that hardly anybody will know that they
are doing so.

What rules has our Church prescribed on the subject? The answer
is, she has given us no rules at all. She bids us fast, each of us according
to our ability, but she does not tell us *how* to do so. Minute rules and
petty distinctions about meats and drinks, could never be of universal
application, and have a great tendency to foster hypocrisy. The Church
would have each individual exercise such an amount of self-denial as
the strength of that individual's constitution will permit. Let each do
according to the ability of each. Let the one who can abstain, do so.
Let the one who cannot abstain, take food of a less palatable or coarser
kind; or if even this is inexpedient, use some other self-denial. Let each
forego some expected pleasure and devote something to God's service

which had been intended for personal use. Let each do something, in short, that is distasteful to them; not, of course, as if there were any *merit* in such a proceeding, but simply by way of become habituated to self-denial, and mastering the corrupt and rebellious will.

Fasting—I cannot repeat it too often—is not an end, but a means, and therefore if we are unable to avail ourselves of this means we should try another. In itself, fasting is nothing; it is only valuable when it helps us to root out sin, and anything which contributes to that design is just as useful as fasting.

"What advantage is it," wrote St. Chrysostom, "if we have kept the fast, and not improved our conduct? If someone tells you, I have fasted the whole of Lent, let your answer be, I had an enemy and am now reconciled; I had a habit of reviling, and have left it off; I had a custom of swearing, and this evil propensity is checked. It is no use for a merchant to cross the seas, unless the merchant returns home laden with goods, nor is there any use in our fasting, if with the act itself, all further good ceases. If our fasting has consisted merely in abstaining from meals, when Lent is ended our fast will have passed away. But if our fast consist in abstaining from sin, when the fast has come to an end the benefit will still remain and will lay up for us treasures in the heavens."

Thus St. Chrysostom puts fasting upon its true principles, according to the light which Scripture had already thrown upon it. For what says the Spirit, by the mouth of the Prophet Isaiah, of the difference between a counterfeit fast and a true one?

"Is such the fast that I choose, a day for a man to humble himself? Is it to bow down his head like a rush, and to spread sackcloth and ashes under him? Will you call this a fast, and a day acceptable to the LORD? Is not this the fast that I choose: to loose the bonds of wickedness, to undo the thongs of the yoke, to let the oppressed go free, and to break every yoke? Is it not to share your bread with the hungry, and bring the homeless poor into your house; when you see the naked, to cover him, and not to hide yourself from your own flesh?

So while fasting is a duty clearly enjoined by the Bible and the Church, its acceptableness with God wholly depends upon the spirit in which it is observed, and the results to which it leads.

Fasting is to help us root out sin.

Wednesday in the First Week of Lent

A reading from *Reflections on Prayer* by Hannah More.

The one to whom the duty of prayer is unknown and by whom the privilege of prayer is unfelt or the one by whom it is neglected or who uses it for form and not from feeling, may well say, "Will this work, wearisome even if necessary, never have an end? Will there be no time when God will dispense with its regular exercise?"

To such a question there is only one answer. If there is any day in which we are quite certain that we shall meet with no trial from Providence, no temptation from the world, any day in which we shall be sure to have no wrong temper aroused in ourselves, no call to bear with those of others, no misfortune to encounter and no need of Divine assistance to endure it, on that morning we may safely omit prayer. If there is any evening in which we have received no protection from God and experienced no mercy at God's hands, if we have not lost a single opportunity of doing or receiving good, if we are quite certain that we have not once spoken unadvisedly with our lips nor entertained one vain or idle thought in our heart, on that night we may safely omit praise to God and the confession of our sinfulness; on that night we may safely omit humiliation and thanksgiving.

When we can conscientiously say that religion has given a tone to our conduct, a law to our actions, a rule to our thoughts, a bridle to our tongue, a restraint to every wrong passion, a check to every evil temper, then some might say we may safely be dismissed from the drudgery of prayer, it will then have served all the purpose which you so tiresomely recommend. So far from it, we really figure to ourselves that if we could hope to hear of a being brought to such perfection of discipline, it would unquestionably be found that this would be the very being who would continue most perseveringly in the practice of that devotion which had so materially contributed to bringing both heart and mind to so desirable a state, who would most tremble to discontinue prayer, who would be most appalled at the thought of the condition to which that one would likely be reduced by such discontinuance.

It is true that those who consider religion something nominal and ceremonial, rather than as a principal of spirit and of life, will feel nothing encouraging, nothing refreshing, nothing delightful in prayer. But those who begin to feel it as the means of procuring the most substantial blessings to the heart; who begin to experience something of the realization of the promises to the soul in the performance of this exercise, will find there is no employment so satisfactory, none that the mind can so little do without, none that so effectually raises them above the world, none that so opens the eyes to its empty shadows, none which can make them look with so much indifference on its lying vanities, none that can so powerfully defend them against the assaults of temptation and the allurements of pleasure, none that can so sustain them in labor, so carry them through difficulties, none that can so quicken them in the practice of every virtue, and animate them in the discharge of every duty.

But if prayer is so exhilarating to the soul, what shall be said of praise? Praise is the only employment, we might almost say it is the only duty, in which self finds no part. In praise we go out of ourselves, and think only of the One to whom we offer it. It is the most purely disinterested of all services. It is gratitude without solicitation, acknowledgment without petition. Prayer is the overflowing expression of our wants, praise of our affections. Prayer is the language of the destitute, praise of the redeemed. If the angelic spirits offer their praises exempt from our infirmity, yet we have a motive for gratitude unknown even to the angels. They are unfallen beings; they cannot say as we can, "Worthy the lamb, who was slain for us."

Prayer is the child of faith, praise of love. Prayer looks forward. Praise takes in, in its wide range, enjoyment of present, remembrance of past and anticipation of future blessings. Prayer points the only way to heaven, praise is already there.

There is nothing so encouraging and refreshing as prayer.

Thursday of the First Week of Lent

A reading on charity from a treatise by Thomas Becon.

God has put the goods of this world into the rich men's hands, that they should distribute part of them to the poor people. They are the stewards of God and dispensers of God's treasures, that those who continually live with them, should also by distributing part of them comfort the needy members of Christ. If they spend them otherwise than God has appointed in God's word, they shall render a strict account for it to Christ the high Judge. They have nothing at all except what they shall be called to account for, even to the uttermost farthing.

If they are not found to have used their talent well, and to the profit of others, they shall, with that unprofitable servant in the gospel, be cast into utter darkness where there shall be weeping and gnashing of teeth. If they are proved unmerciful and negligent in the distribution of worldly goods, surely they shall be carried with the rich glutton, of whom blessed Luke speaks in the gospel, into hell, and there burn in such cruel and bitter flames that its fire shall never be quenched, "neither shall the worm," which shall gnaw the consciences of those who are there. What cause then have the rich to boast themselves and to glory in their worldly goods, or to advance themselves above others for the sake of their possessions? Certainly, none at all; no more than a great man's servant has to whom the lord and master has committed goods for a certain space to keep, the servant looking at every hour to see when that master will call the servant to account and require them back again.

Basil the Great, in a notable sentence, says this: "That one is a true thief, a robber," says he, "who makes that thing his or her own that was received in order to distribute it and give it abroad. For the bread that you retain and keep is the bread of the hungry; the garment which you keep in your chest is the garment of the naked; the shoe that is moldy with you is the shoe of one who is unshod; and the money which you hide in the ground is the money of the needy. Moreover you do injury and plain wrong to as many as you forsake, when you are able to help them."

The saying of the wise man applies here: "The bread of the needy is the life of the poor: whoever defrauds them of it is a murderer." God also by the prophet teaches us that the fast that pleases God best is accompanied with works of mercy, saying, "Break your bread to the hungry, and lead the needy and wayfaring into your house. When you see those who are naked, cover them; and do not despise your flesh." Notice that he says: "Break your bread to the hungry." There are some who expound this text to say that you do break your bread to the hungry when you fast in such a way that you spare from your own belly to give to the poor and hungry. For a Christian ought to be no less careful for the poor than for the self. We therefore do break our bread to the hungry, when we give them that which we ourselves would have eaten.

To break our bread to the hungry, to lodge the poor in our house, to give clothes to the naked, and to comfort according to our ability as many as have need of our help: to these works of mercy our Savior Christ exhorts us in the gospel, saying: "When you make dinner or a supper, do not call your friends, nor your relatives, nor your kinsfolk, nor your rich neighbors; lest they also invite you in turn, and a recompense be made. But when you make a feast, call the poor, the feeble, the lame, and the blind; and you shall be happy; for they cannot repay you; but you shall be repaid at the resurrection of the righteous" (Luke 14:12–14).

The bread you keep is the bread of the hungry.

Friday of the First Week of Lent

A meditation on the cross from *Poems, Centuries, and Three Thanksgivings* by Thomas Traherne.

Lord Jesus, what love shall I render to you, for your love to me, your eternal love! Oh what fervor, what ardor, what humiliation, what reverence, what joy, what adoration, what zeal, what thanksgiving! You are perfect in beauty, you are the king of eternal glory, you reign in the highest heavens and yet came down from heaven to die for me! And shall not I live for you? O my joy! O my sovereign friend! O my life, and my all! I beseech you to let those trickling drops of blood that run down your flesh drop upon me. O let your love inflame me: love so deep and infinite, that you suffered the wrath of God for me, and purchased all nations and kingdoms to be my treasures; you redeemed me from hell, and when you had overcome the sharpness of death you opened the kingdom of heaven to all believers; What shall I do for you?

What shall I do for you, O preserver of all: live, love, and admire; and learn to become such to you as you are to me. O glorious soul, whose comprehensive understanding at once contains all kingdoms and ages! O glorious mind, whose love extends to all creatures! O miraculous and eternal God-head, now suffering on the cross for me:

Why, Lord Jesus, do you love us, why are we your treasures? What wonder is this, that you should esteem us so as to die for us? Show me the reasons of your love, that I may love all others too. O goodness ineffable! they are the treasures of your goodness who so infinitely love them that you gave yourself for them. Your goodness delighted to be communicated to them whom you had saved. O you who are most glorious in goodness, make me abundant in this goodness like yourself, that I may as deeply pity others' misery, and as ardently thirst for their happiness as you do. Let the same mind be in me that is in Christ Jesus, for those who are not led by the Spirit of Christ are none of his. Holy Jesus, I admire your love; I admire your love to me also. O that I could see it through all those wounds! O that I could feel it in all those stripes! O that I could hear it in all those groans! O that I could taste it beneath that gall and vinegar! O that I could smell the savor of thy sweet ointments, even in this Golgotha or Place of a Skull. I pray you to teach me first your love to me, and then to all mankind! But in your love to mankind I am beloved.

These wounds are in themselves openings too small to let in my sight, to the vast comprehension of your eternal love. These wounds engraved in your hands are only shady impressions; unless I see the glory of your soul, in which the fulness of the God-head dwells bodily. These bloody characters are too dim to let me read it, in its luster and perfection till I see your person and know your ways! O you that hang upon this cross before my eyes, whose face is bleeding, and covered over with tears and filth and blows! Angels adore the glory of your God-head in the highest heavens who in every thought, and in every work did glorious things for me from everlasting! What could I, O my Lord, desire more then such a world! Such heavens and such an earth, such beasts and fowls and fishes made for me! All these do homage to me, and I have dominion over them from the beginning! The heavens and the earth minister to me, as if no one were created but I alone. I willingly acknowledge it to be your gift, your bounty to me! How many thousand ways do others also minister to me! O what riches have you prepared out of nothing for me! All creatures labor for my sake, and I am made to enjoy all your creatures. O what praises shall I return to you, the wisdom of the Creator and the brightness of the glory of the eternal goodness, who made all for me before you redeemed me.

Shall I not live for you?

Saturday of the First Week of Lent

A reading from a sermon on baptism by Thomas Cranmer.

Our Lord Jesus Christ, good children, in the Gospel of St. John, says this: "No one can enter the kingdom of God without being born of water and Spirit." Now we ought to direct our whole life to come to the kingdom of heaven. For the Lord saith, "Seek first the kingdom of God" (Matthew 6:33, KJV). And you have heard before this that we daily make this petition to God, "Thy kingdom come." Therefore it is very necessary for us to know how we must be born again, and what this second birth is, without which we cannot enter into the kingdom of God. But when we speak of a second birth, you shall not so badly understand this saying, as though someone, who is born once, should enter again into his mother's womb, and so be born again as he was before. It would be very foolish to think that. But here we mean a second birth which is spiritual, by which our inward self and mind is renewed by the Holy Spirit, so that our hearts and minds receive new desires, which they did not have from their first birth or nativity.

And the second birth is by the water of baptism, which Paul calls the bath of regeneration, because our sins are forgiven us in baptism, and the Holy Spirit is poured into us as into God's beloved children, so that by the power and working of the Holy Spirit we are born again spiritually, and made new creatures. And so by baptism we enter into the kingdom of God, and shall be saved for ever, if we continue to our lives' end in the faith of Christ.

Therefore, good children, consider diligently the strength of baptism, and mark well what great treasures and what excellent benefits you received in your baptism, that you may thank God for the same, and strengthen yourselves by them in all your temptations, and endeavor yourselves faithfully to perform all things which you promised in your baptism. And that you may do this better, hear and learn the words of our master Christ, by which he ordained and instituted baptism, and often repeat the same, so that you may learn them word for word without the book. These be the words of our Lord Jesus Christ, spoken to his disciples: "Go therefore and make disciples of all nations, baptizing them in the name of the Father and of the Son and of the Holy Spirit." "The one who believes and is baptized will be saved; but the one who does not believe will be condemned."

By these words our Lord Jesus Christ instituted baptism, by which we are born again to the kingdom of God. And you, good children, shall give diligence not only to rehearse these words, but also to understand what Christ meant by the same; so that when you are asked any question, you may both make a direct answer, and also in time to come be able to teach your children, as you yourselves are now instructed. For what greater shame can there be than for some to profess themselves to be Christians because they are baptized, and yet they do not know what baptism is, nor what strength it has, nor what the dipping in the water betokens? But all our lifetime we ought to keep those promises, which we solemnly made there before God and other Christians; and all our profession and life ought to agree to our baptism.

For I want you to know this well, good children, that those who are baptized may assuredly say this—I am not now in this wavering opinion that I only suppose myself to be a Christian. For I know for a surety that I am baptized, and I am sure also that baptism was ordained of God, and that the one who baptized me did it by God's commission and commandment. And the Holy Spirit bears witness that the one who is baptized has put on Christ. Therefore the Holy Spirit in my baptism assures me, that I am a Christian. And this is a true and sincere faith which is able to stand against the gates of hell, because it has the evidence of God's word, and does not lean on anyone's saying or opinion.

My baptism assures me that I am a Christian.

The Second Week of Lent

Weigh all my faults and follies righteously,
    Omissions and commissions, sin on sin;
    Make deep the scale, O Lord, to weigh them in;
Yea, set the Accuser vulture-eyed to see
All loads ingathered which belong to me;
    That so in life the judgment may begin,
    And all may learn how hard it is to win
One solitary sinful soul to Thee.
I have no merits for a counterpoise:
    Oh vanity my work and hastening day,
What can I answer to the accusing voice?
    Lord, drop Thou in the counterscale alone
  One Drop from Thine own Heart, and overweigh
    My guilt, my folly, even my heart of stone.

–Christina Rossetti

The Second Sunday in Lent

A reading on love from *Christus Veritas* by William Temple.

In thinking of God, as Christians have learned to believe in God, the mind is always free; it is the finite before the Infinite, but its freedom proves its kinship. We are God's children, and cannot fully understand God, but God is our Father, and we know God enough to love God. As we love God we learn, for God's sake and in God's power, to love others. So loving, we become partakers of the Divine Nature, sharers in that divine activity whereby God is God.

Thus nothing falls outside the circle of the Divine Love. The structure of Reality is the articulate expression of Divine Love. God loves; God answers with love; and the love wherewith God loves and answers is God: Three Persons, One God.

God is Love. But we miss the full wonder and glory of that supreme revelation if we let the term Love, as we naturally understand it, supply the whole meaning of the term God. There is a great danger lest we forget the Majesty of God, and so think of God's love as a mere amiability. We must first realize God as exalted in unapproachable Holiness, so that our only fitting attitude before God is one of abject self-abasement, if we are to feel the stupendous marvel of the Love which led God, so high and lifted up, to take a place beside us in our insignificance and squalor that we might be united with God's self. "When I look at your heavens, the work of your fingers, the moon and the stars that you have established; what are human beings that you are mindful of them, mortals that you care for them?"

To omit the thought of God's majesty, and to rebel at language of self-abasement in God's presence, is not only to cut at the historic and psychological root of all human religion, but it defeats its own object, for it belittles the Love which it seeks to enhance. If our first thought of God is that God always has a welcome for us, there is less thrill of wonder in that welcome than if we first remember God's Eternity and Holiness, and then pass to the confident conviction, which remains a mystery commanding silent awe—"our fellowship is with the Father."

But no; it does not merely remain such a mystery; this is itself the climax of mystery, which we apprehend (if at all) in an agony of joy and a rapture of fear. For the joy is shot through with the sense of our unworthiness, the rapture intensifies the fear that is our response to overwhelming greatness. So it is only half the truth to say that we must worship the Transcendent in order to appreciate the Immanent. God is never so transcendent as when God is most immanent. It was in the consciousness that he came from God and went to God that our Lord performed the act of menial service. It was when he acknowledged his earthly Name that the very soldiers went backward and fell to the ground. Nor is there any more august and awe-inspiring symbol of the supremacy of the Most High than the sublime and dreadful solitude of the figure on the Cross—a spiritual loneliness made more intense by the physical proximity of dying malefactors and mocking crowds, for whom in his agony he prayed.

"This is the true God and eternal life."

Nothing falls outside the circle of the divine love.

Monday of the Second Week of Lent

A reading from a sermon by Mark Frank on the text, "I punish my body and enslave it, so that after proclaiming to others I myself should not be disqualified" (1 Corinthians 9:27).

If the first preachers of the Gospel, the grand Apostles, those stars and angels of the churches, must deal so roughly with their bodies, for fear of being "disqualified," who is it can dream that they are exempt? If the strongest cedars shake, what shall the reeds do? Unless you "mortify the deeds of the body," (it is to all of us it is said) there is no living. If we keep not our bodies low, they will keep us low; if we bring them not into subjection, they will bring us into slavery.

Nor is it so hard a business as some would seem to make it. We can sit up whole nights to game, to dance, to revel, to see a mask or play, and make nothing of it. We can rise up early and go to bed late, for months together, for our gain and profit, and be never the worse. We can fast whole days together, and not eat or drink, when we are eager upon our business or sport, and never feel it. We can endure pain and cold, affronts and injuries and neglects, slightings and reproaches too, to compass a little honor and preferment, and not say a word. Only the soul's business is not worth the while; whether "disqualified" or no, is not worth considering; all is too much on that account: mole-hills are mountains, and there is a lion always in the way—watching will kill us, fasting will destroy us, any kind of strictness will impair us; temperance itself will pine us into skeletons; every good exercise takes up too much time; every petty thing that crosses the way is an unconquerable difficulty, a lion—when the soul's business is to be gone about.

But suppose you are infirm, indeed, and can not do so much as perhaps you would do otherwise, can you do nothing? If you can not watch, can you not fast sometimes? If you can not fast, can you not endure a little hunger, thirst, or cold, or pains, for heaven either? If all these seem hard, can you not be temperate either? can you not bring yourself to it by degrees, by exercise, and practice either? Or if you can not watch a night, can you not watch an hour—do somewhat towards it? If you can not fast from all kinds of meat, can you not abstain at least from some—from dainties and delicacies? If not often, can you not at such a time as this, when all Christians ever used to do it? Surely the one who cannot fast a meal, may yet feed upon coarser fare. The one who cannot do any of these for long, may do all of them for some time; may exercise in a little time to the hardest of them all. Let us, then, however, set to doing something; for God's sake let us be Christians a little at the least; let us do somewhat that is akin to the ancient piety—watch, or fast, or somewhat, in some degree or other— that the world may believe that we are Christians. Why should we be "disqualified"?

But I must not end with so sad a word. All that has been said is not that any should be disqualified. It is in our hands to hinder it: it is but a few hours taken from our sleep and employed on heaven, it is but a little taken from our full dishes and groaning tables and bestowed upon the poor, it is but the keeping of the body under and the soul in awe and all is safe. The holy fear of being disqualified shall keep you safe from ever being so. The bringing of the body into subjection here shall bring it hereafter into a kingdom where all our fears shall be turned into joys, our fasting into feasting, our watching into rest, and these very corruptible bodies shall be raised into incorruption where we shall meet the full reward of all our pains and labors, the everlasting crown of righteousness, the incorruptible and eternal crown of glory.

The work of discipline is in our hands.

Tuesday of the Second Week of Lent

A reading on fasting from a sermon by Phillips Brooks
on the text: "And whenever you fast, do not look dismal,
like the hypocrites, for they disfigure their faces so as to
show others that they are fasting. Truly I tell you, they
have received their reward. But when you fast, put oil on
your head and wash your face, so that your fasting may
be seen not by others but by your Father who is in secret;
and your Father who sees in secret will reward you"
(Matthew 6:16–18).

The idea of Lent is spiritual culture, and always, as a part of that idea, has been associated with Lent the idea of abstinence. We are looking forward to a soberer and quieter life, a life which in some form or other is to fast from some of its indulgences. Is it not good that we should try to see what God designs by those Lents, those periods of sobered life and abstinence from outward pleasures, which both in God's word and in the intimations of our own nature have God's sanction and authority?

God has a reason for everything. Our best religious progress consists in large part of this, the coming by sympathy with God to see the reasons of what have been to us bare commandments. The change from the arbitrary to the essential look in what God does is the richest and most delightful feature of the spiritual growth.

Let us ask what is the use of fasting, for so we shall best come to understand the true methods and degrees of fasting. And let us begin with this. All bodily discipline, all voluntary abstinence from pleasure of whatever sort, must be of value either as a symbol of something or as a means of something. These two functions belong to it as being connected with the body, which is at once the utterer and the educator of the soul within.

Just suppose any great mental or moral change to come in someone's life. We will not speak of the great fundamental religious change of conversion; but any change from frivolity to earnestness, from lightness to seriousness of life. The one who has been careless, free, and irresponsible, taking life as it came, with no reality, no sense of duty, undertakes a different way of living, begins to study, begins to work, seeks knowledge, accepts obligations. The old life fades away and a new life begins. Self-indulgence is put aside. Self-devotion takes its place. This is a spiritual, an inward change. It is independent of outward circumstances. One may conceivably live this new life, and everything external be still the same that it has always been. But practically this more earnest inward life suits the outer life to itself. Quickly or gradually the one who has begun to live more seriously within, begins to live more simply without. Such a one comes instinctively to less gorgeous dresses and barer walls and slighter feasts. The outer life is restrained and simplified. And this restraint and simplicity is at once a symbol or expression of the changed inner life, and a means for its cultivation.

If the change is one which involves repentance and self-reproach, the giving up of a life which never ought to have been lived at all for one that always has been a duty, then both of these offices of the outward self-denial become plainer. The stripping of the old luxury off from the life is at once an utterance of humble regret for a wrong past, and also an opening of the soul to new and better influences. It is as when a reveler at a banquet is suddenly summoned to a battle where he ought to be in the front rank. As he springs up from the couch in self-reproach, the casting away of his garlands and his robes means, first, his shame at having been idle and feasting when he ought to have been at work; and second, his eagerness to have his limbs free so that the work which he has now undertaken may be well done. His stripping off of his wanton luxuries is at once a symbol of his self-reproach for the past, and a means of readiness for the new work that awaits him. And that is the meaning of all voluntary mortification which has any meaning.

Fasting provides an opening of the soul.

Wednesday of the Second Week of Lent

A reading on "The Prayer Life of Jesus" from *Footsteps of the Master* by Harriet Beecher Stowe.

Now there are many good people whose feeling about prayer is something like this: "I pray because I am commanded to, not because I feel a special need or find a special advantage in it." In my view we are to use our intellect and our will in discovering duties and overcoming temptations, quite sure that God will, of course, aid those who aid themselves. This class of persons looks upon all protracted seasons of prayer and seasons spent in devotion as so much time taken from the active duties of life. A week devoted to prayer, a convention of Christians meeting to spend eight or ten days in exercises purely devotional, would strike them as something excessive and unnecessary, and tending to fanaticism.

If ever there was a human being who could be supposed able to meet the trials of life and overcome its temptations in his own strength, it must have been Jesus Christ. But his example stands out among all others, and he is shown to us as peculiarly a man of prayer.

If Jesus Christ deemed so much time spent in prayer needful to his work, what shall we say of ourselves? Feeble and earthly, with hearts always prone to go astray, living in a world where everything presses us downward to the lower regions of the senses and possessions, how can we afford to neglect that higher communion, those seasons of divine solitude, which were thought necessary by our Master? It was in those many days devoted entirely to communion with God that he gained strength to resist the temptations of Satan before which we so often fall.

The Christian Church felt so greatly the need of definite seasons devoted to religious retirement that there grew up among them the custom now so extensively observed in Christendom of devoting forty days in every year to a special retirement from things of earth and a special devotion to the work of private and public prayer. Like all customs, even those originating in deep spiritual influences, this is too apt to degenerate into a mere form. Many associate no ideas with "fasting" except a change in articles of food. The true spiritual fasting, which consists of turning our eyes and hearts from the engrossing cares and pleasures of earth and fixing them on things divine, is lost sight of. Our "forty days" are not like our Lord's, given to prayer and the study of God's Word. Nothing could make the period of Lent so much of a reality as to employ it in a systematic effort to fix the mind on Jesus. The history in the Gospels is so well worn that it often slips through the head without affecting the heart.

But if, retiring into solitude for a portion of each day, we should select some one scene or trait or incident in the life of Jesus, and with all the helps we can get seek to understand it fully, tracing it in the other evangelists, comparing it with other passages of scripture etc., we should find ourselves insensibly interested, and might hope that in this effort of our souls to understand him, Jesus himself would draw near, as he did to the disciples on the way to Emmaus.

This looking into Jesus and thinking about him is a better way to meet and overcome sin than any spiritual austerities or spiritual self-reproaches. It is by looking at him, the apostle says, "as though reflected in a mirror," that we are "transformed into the same image from one degree of glory to another."

Prayer is to transform us into the image of Jesus.

Thursday of the Second Week of Lent

A reading on Christian charity from *A Serious Call to a Devout and Holy Life* by William Law.

As the holiness of Christianity consecrates all states and employments of life to God, as it requires us to do and use every thing as the servants of God, so are we more specially obliged to observe this religious exactness in the use of our estates and fortunes.

The reason for this would appear very plain, if we were only to consider that our estate is as much the gift of God as our eyes or our hands, and is no more to be buried or thrown away at pleasure, than we are to put out our eyes, or throw away our limbs as we please.

But besides this consideration, there are several other great and important reasons why we should be religiously exact in the use of our estates.

First, because the manner of using our money or spending our estate enters so far into the business of every day, and makes so great a part of our common life, that our common life must be much of the same nature as our common way of spending our estate. If reason and religion govern us in this, then reason and religion have got great hold of us; but if humor, pride, and fancy are the measures of our spending our estate, then humor, pride, and fancy will have the direction of the greatest part of our life.

Secondly, another great reason for devoting all our estate to right uses is this: because it is capable of being used to the most excellent purposes, and is so great a means of doing good. If we waste it we do not waste a trifle that signifies little, but we waste that which might be made as eyes to the blind, as a husband to the widow, as a father to the orphan; we waste that which not only enables us to minister worldly comforts to those who are in distress, but that which might purchase for ourselves everlasting treasures in heaven. So that if we part with our money in foolish ways, we part with a great power of comforting our fellow-creatures, and of making ourselves for ever blessed.

If there be nothing so glorious as doing good, if there is nothing that makes us so like to God, then nothing can be so glorious in the use of our money, as to use it all in works of love and goodness, making ourselves friends and benefactors to all our fellow-creatures, imitating the divine love, and turning all our power into acts of generosity, care, and kindness to such as are in need of it.

If we had eyes, and hands, and feet that we could give to those who needed them; if we should either lock them up in a chest, or please ourselves with some needless or ridiculous use of them, instead of giving them to our neighbors that are blind and lame, should we not justly be reckoned as inhuman wretches? If we should instead choose to amuse ourselves with furnishing our houses with those things, rather than to entitle ourselves to an eternal reward by giving them to those that wanted eyes and hands, might we not justly be reckoned as mad?

Now money has very much the nature of eyes and feet; if we either lock it up in chests, or waste it in needless and ridiculous expenses upon ourselves, while the poor and the distressed want it for their necessary uses; if we consume it in the ridiculous ornaments of apparel while others are starving in nakedness we are not far from the cruelty of one who chooses rather to adorn the house with the hands and eyes than to give them to those that want them. If I choose to indulge myself in such expensive enjoyments as have no real use in them, such as satisfy no real want, rather than to entitle myself to an eternal reward, by disposing of my money well, I am guilty of this madness, that rather chooses to lock up eyes and hands, than to make myself for ever blessed by giving them to those who want them. For after we have satisfied our own sober and reasonable wants, all the rest of our money is something that can only be used well by giving it to those that need it.

Nothing makes us so like God as to use our money in works of love.

Friday of the Second Week of Lent

A reading on the cross from a sermon by Charles Kingsley on the text: "I pray that you may have the power to comprehend, with all the saints, what is the breadth and length and height and depth, and to know the love of Christ that surpasses knowledge, so that you may be filled with all the fullness of God" (Ephesians 3:18–19).

St. Paul calls the cross a mystery—a secret—which had been hidden from the foundation of the world, and he says his great hope was this—to make people know the love of Christ; to look at Christ's cross, and take in its breadth, and length, and depth, and height. It passes knowledge, he says. We shall never know the whole of it, but the more we know of it, the more blessed and hopeful, the more strong and earnest, the more good and righteous we shall become.

And what is the breadth of Christ's cross? My friends, it is as broad as the whole world; for he died for the whole world, as it is written, "He is a propitiation not for our sins only, but for the sins of the whole world"; and again, "God wills that none should perish."

And what is the length of Christ's cross? The length, says an early Christian writer, signifies the time during which its virtue will last. How long, then, is the cross of Christ? Long enough to last through all time. As long as there is a sinner to be saved; as long as there is ignorance, sorrow, pain, death, or anything else which is contrary to God and hurtful to us in the universe of God, so long will Christ's cross last. For it is written, he must reign till he has put all enemies under his feet; and God is all in all.

And how high is Christ's cross? As high as the highest heaven, for when Christ hung upon the cross, heaven came down on earth, and earth ascended into heaven. Christ never showed forth his Father's glory so perfectly as when, hanging upon the cross, he cried in his death-agony, "Father, forgive them; for they know not what they do." Those words showed the true height of the cross, and caused St. John to know that his vision was true, and no dream, when he saw afterwards in the midst of the throne of God a lamb standing as if it had been slaughtered.

And how deep is the cross of Christ? This is a great mystery, and one which people in these days are afraid to look at; and darken it of their own will, because they will neither believe their Bibles, nor the voice of their own hearts.

But if the cross of Christ is as high as heaven, then, it seems to me, it must also be as deep as hell, deep enough to reach the deepest sinner in the deepest pit to which he may fall. We know that Christ descended into hell. We know that he preached to the spirits in prison. We know that it is written, "As in Adam all die, even so in Christ shall all be made alive." We know that God does not have one law for one of us and another for another, or one law for one year, and another for another. It is possible, therefore, that God has not one law for this life, and another for the life to come. Let us hope, then, that David's words may be true after all, when speaking by the Spirit of God, he says, not only, "if I ascend up to heaven, you are there" but "if I go down to hell, you are there also"; and let us hope that *that* is the depth of the cross of Christ.

At all events, my friends, I believe that we shall find St. Paul's words true, when he says, that Christ's love passes knowledge: and therefore that we shall find this also—that however broad we may think Christ's cross, it is broader still. However long, it is longer still. However high, it is higher still. However deep, it is deeper still. Yes, we shall find that St. Paul spoke solemn truth when he said, that Christ had ascended on high that he might fill all things; that Christ filled all in all; and that he must reign till the day when he shall give up the kingdom to God, even the Father, that God may be all in all.

To know the love of Christ is to look at Christ's cross.

Saturday of the Second Week of Lent

A reading concerning baptism from a sermon by
Charles Kingsley entitled "The Message of Christ to
the Working Man."

ook again at baptism—a sacrament or sign—and what a
sign! Thoughtless people have sneered at it for its simplicity,
and laughed at the church for attributing, as they say, miraculous virtues to the sprinkling of a little water, as if the very simplicity
of the sign was not in itself a gospel, that is, good news to the poor,
proclaiming that baptism is the witness of a blessing not meant merely
for the high-born, or the philosopher, or the genius, but, like the rain
of heaven and the running brook, free to all, even to the poorest and
to the most degraded: our right, as water is, simply because we are
human beings.

Baptism works no miracle; it proclaims a miracle which has been
from all eternity. It proclaims that we are members of Christ, children
of God, citizens of a spiritual kingdom—that is, of a kingdom of love,
justice, self-sacrifice, freedom, equality. Those spiritual laws, says baptism, are the true ground and constitution of all human society, and
not rank, force, wealth, expediency, or any outward material ground
whatsoever; not they, but the Kingdom of God whose name is Love
and Righteousness, which, if any nation or society seek first, all other
outward and material blessings of health, wealth, and civilization will
be surely added to them, because they will be working in harmony
with the laws of the one who made the world of matter, as well as the
laws of spirit.

To take a single instance of what I mean—what is the plain and
simple meaning of the baptismal sign, but washing—purification—

and that alike of the child of the queen and the child of the beggar? It testifies of the right of each, because the will of God for each is that they should be pure. And what better witness do you want, my friends, against that vile neglect which allows tens of thousands in our great cities to grow up hogs in body, soul, and spirit? If we really believe the meaning of that baptismal sign, we should need few further arguments in favor of sanitary reform, for the very poorest outcasts would feel that they had a right to say, God's will is that my children should be pure washed without and within from everything that denies and degrades humanity, my child is God's child—God's spirit is with it. It is the temple of the Living God, and whosoever defiles the temple of God, God will destroy. God has promised to purify its spirit: how dare you interfere with God's work? God's will is that its whole body, soul, and spirit, should be preserved blameless, and grow up to the full stature of a noble humanity.

How dare you stand in the way of the will of God towards even one of the meanest of God's creatures? How dare you, in your sectarian jealousy, your dread of that light which after all comes down from God, who is the Father of Light; how dare you, I say, refuse to allow this child's mind to be purified by education; how dare you, for the sake of your own private greed or party chicaneries, refuse to allow this child's body such purity as God has not denied even to the wild beast in his native forest? How dare you, in the face of that baptismal sign of the sprinkled water, keep God's children exposed to the filth, brutality, and temptation which festers in your courts and alleys, making cleanliness impossible—drunkenness all but excusable—prostitution all but natural—self-respect and decency unknown?

I speak the truth of God. In that font is a witness for education and for sanitary reform, which will conquer with the might of an archangel, when every other argument has failed to prove that the masses are after all not mere machines and hands to be used up in the production of a wealth of which they never taste, when their numbers are, as far as possible, kept down by economical and prudent rulers, to the market demand for—members of Christ, children of God, and inheritors of the Kingdom of Heaven.

Baptism proclaims that we are citizens of a spiritual kingdom.

The Third Week of Lent

True Lent

Is this a fast, to keep
The larder lean,
and clean
From fat of veal and sheep?

Is it to quit the dish
Of flesh, yet still
To fill
The platter high with fish?

Is it to fast an hour,
Or ragged to go,
Or show
A downcast look, and sour?

No; 'tis a fast to dole
Thy sheaf of wheat
And meat
Unto the hungry soul.

It is to fast from strife,
From old debate
And hate;
To circumcise thy life;

To show a heart grief-rent;
To starve they sin,
Not bin.
And that's to keep thy Lent.

–Robert Herrick, 1647

The Third Sunday in Lent

A reading from a sermon by Edward B. Pusey on love.

Love, as Holy Scripture speaks of it, is the love of God for God's self above all things, and of humanity for God and in God. It shows itself in outward acts of love to humanity, or, where it may be, in labor for God. But these are only outward forms, in which the inward life expresses itself. These shall cease in the world to come (for where there is no misery, there is no room for works of mercy, nor for labor where all is everlasting rest), but "Love never fails." It is itself deep within, in the heart, always there when not called to act, like hot glowing coals, which dart forth in a quick consuming flame when fuel is laid upon them, but their deep, pure, white heat is within.

Acts of love strengthen the inward fire of love; and love, which does not express itself in deeds of love, would go out, as fire without fuel. But they do not first light it. Love is the "fire," which our Blessed Lord "came to bring . . . to the earth," and wished "it were already kindled!" He kindled it by his own death and passion, "heaping coals of fire upon our heads," to melt us into love. He kindled it, by sending his Spirit into our hearts, "a Spirit of burning" to burn out what was defiled, enlighten what was dark, make what was cold to glow, melt what was stone, purging away our dross and changing the dull ore into the fine gold. "Love is of God," and "God is Love." In God, Love is the self, the very substance, the very bond of unity of the Co-equal Trinity. For "God is Love." In angels and humanity, love is the gift of God, given to us by the one who is the gift of God, "shed abroad in our hearts by the Holy Spirit who is given to us." "Love gives love." God "who is love, gives the Spirit" who is love, to pour abroad love into our hearts. Love then is the source and end of all good. "It alone," says Augustine, "distinguishes the children of God from the children of the devil."

Without love, nothing avails; with it, you have all things. If it were possible that, without it, you could "have all faith, so as to remove mountains," the Apostle says, you are "nothing." Judas cast out devils, we must suppose; but he was himself a devil. He was nothing, for he had not the life of God; he was but a blot in God's Creation. Without love, all knowledge of divine things is ignorance; all eloquence, though it were the speech of Angels, "a tinkling cymbal," hollow and empty, for it is not filled by God.

Without love, all gifts to the poor, all zeal for the honor of God, yes, to suffer death, if it were possible, for the Name of Jesus, would profit nothing. With love, the cup of cold water given for Jesus' sake, or the two mites, are rich, acceptable gifts, and the mute longing of the soul pleads eloquently for the conversion of sinners; and unlearned and ignorant people speak with the Spirit of Christ; and the weak things of the world overcome the mighty, and children trample on Satan, the prince of this world; and "things which are not, bring to nought things which are," since they are filled and strengthened and ensouled and empowered by the One who alone IS and is love.

With love, you have all things.

Monday of the Third Week of Lent

A reading on discipline from *Earthly Care* by
Harriet Beecher Stowe.

The Bible tells us that our whole existence here is *disciplinary*;
that this whole physical system, by which our spirit is connected with all the joys and sorrows, hopes and fears, and
wants which form a part of it, is designed as an education to fit the
soul for its immortality. Hence, as worldly cares form the greater part
of every human life, there must be some mode of viewing and meeting it, which converts it from an enemy of spirituality into a means of
grace and spiritual advancement.

How then shall earthly care become heavenly discipline? How shall
the disposition of the weight be altered so as to press the spirit upwards
toward God instead of downward and away? How shall the pillar of
cloud which rises between us and God become one of fire, to reflect
upon us constantly the light of God's countenance and to guide us
over the sands of life's desert?

It appears to us that the great radical difficulty lies in a wrong
belief. There is not a genuine and real belief of the presence and agency
of God in the minor events and details of life, which is necessary to
change them from secular cares into spiritual blessings.

When the breath of slander or the pressure of human injustice
comes so heavily on us as really to threaten loss of character and
destruction of temporal interests, we seem forced to recognize the
hand and voice of God through the veil of human agencies, but the
smaller injustice and fault-finding which meet everyone in the daily
intercourse of life, these daily-recurring sources of disquietude and
unhappiness are not referred to God's providence, nor considered as a
part of God's probation and discipline. Those thousand vexations
which come upon us through the unreasonableness, the carelessness,

the various constitutional failings or ill-adaptedness of others to our peculiarities of character, form a very large item of the disquietudes of life; and yet how few look beyond the human agent and feel that these are trials coming from God!

Hence too arise a coldness and generality and wandering of mind in prayer. The things that are on the heart, that are distracting the mind, that have filled the heart so full that there is no room for anything else, are all considered too small and undignified to come within the pale of a prayer; and so with a wandering mind and a distracted heart Christians offer up their prayer for things which they think they *ought* to want and make no mention of those which they really *do* want. We pray that God would pour out the Spirit on the heathen, and convert the world, and build up the kingdom everywhere, when perhaps a whole set of little anxieties and wants and vexations are so distracting our thoughts that we hardly know what we are saying. But all this trouble forms no subject-matter for prayer though it is all the while lying like lead on the heart and keeping it down so that it has no power to expand and take in anything else. But were God in Christ known and regarded as the soul's familiar friend; were it felt that even the smallest of life's troubles has been permitted for specific good purpose to the soul, how much more heart work there would be in prayer! how constant, how daily it might become! how it might settle and clear the atmosphere of the soul! how it might dispose and lay away many anxieties which now take up their place.

But to the Christian who really believes in the agency of God in the smallest events of life, confides in God's love, and makes God's sympathy a refuge, the thousand minute cares and perplexities of life become each one a fine affiliating bond between the soul and its God. Christ is known, not by abstract definition, but known as we know our friends. And as we go on thus year by year, and find in every changing situation, in every reverse, in every trouble, from the lightest sorrow to those which wring our soul from its depths, that God is equally present, and that God's gracious aid is equally adequate, our faith seems gradually almost to change to sight, and Christ's sympathy, his love and care, seem to us more real than any other source of reliance; and multiplied cares and trials are only new avenues of acquaintance between us and Heaven.

Christ is the soul's familiar friend.

Tuesday of the Third Week of Lent

A reading on fasting from a sermon by William Beveridge on the text: "but I punish my body and enslave it, so that after proclaiming to others I myself should not be disqualified" (1 Corinthians 9:27).

The keeping of the body under by fasting and so bringing it into subjection to the soul, contributes very much to the exercise of all true holiness.

Are you addicted to pride? Although there is a spiritual pride which degenerate souls are subject to, as well as fallen angels, yet that which mostly puffs up mankind with vain and foolish conceits of themselves usually springs from the corruption of the fancy, caused by those malign vapors, which by reason of too much eating are exhaled from the stomach into the head and there disturb the imagination. But fasting prevents the very engendering of such fumes, and by consequence the corruption of the fancy by them so that the mind is able to judge things as they are, and to see clearly that we neither have nor can have anything in the world to be proud of, but many things to be humbled for; and therefore the keeping the body under, is certainly the best way in the world to keep the mind humble and lowly.

Are you inclined to covetousness? To dote upon the toys and trifles of this lower world? This also must be ascribed very much to the depraved imagination, representing these little things as in a magnifying glass, and so making them seem to be what they really are not and therefore as fasting frees the imagination from all that corrupts it, so it must help to the mind's looking at things as it were with its naked eye, and so passing a right judgment upon them, by which means it is soon brought to condemn and despise the world as much as ever it admired or loved it.

Are you dull and heavy at your devotions, not able to pray, to hear, to meditate, or serve the Lord without distractions? Whence comes that dullness? Whence these distractions but from that hurry of gross vapors in the brain, which obstruct its passages and crowd about it so disorderly, that the soul cannot without much time and pains bring them together, and reduce them to order, so as to make any tolerable use of them? And therefore as these distractions are caused by overmuch eating, so they may be cured by fasting.

So it is that any of you may find by experience that you can never perform any spiritual exercise with that life and vigor, that cheerfulness and alacrity, that constant presence and composure of mind, as when your bodies are empty, and so kept under as to be in a due subjection to the soul.

But the great and principal reason of all why fasting so contributes to true holiness is that fasting is so pleasing and acceptable to Almighty God, that God has promised a blessing, a reward to it, whenever it is rightly performed, and that too not by the mouth of a Prophet, an Apostle, or an Angel, but by his own divine mouth when he was here upon earth. For Our Lord himself says, "When you fast, put oil on your head and wash your face, so that your fasting may be seen not by others but by your Father who is in secret; and your Father who sees in secret will reward you." From which it is plain, that if someone does not fast out of vain ostentation to be seen of others and thought holy, but out of a sincere design to keep the body under, and be better fit for the service of God, that one shall certainly be rewarded for it. But what reward shall we have? Why, God will bless and sanctify it to the great ends and purposes for which it is designed. Fasting, as I have shown, does contribute much to our being holy, but it cannot make us so; that is only in the power of God, the only fountain of all true grace and holiness. But God being well pleased with fasting, where it is duly observed, does by grace and the Spirit make it effectual for the subduing our lusts and for our performance of all holy and good works.

God is well pleased with fasting.

Wednesday of the Third Week of Lent

A reading from *The Spirit of Prayer* by William Law.

The Spirit of Prayer is a pressing forth of the soul out of this earthly life. It is a stretching with all its desire after the life of God. It is a leaving, as far as it can, all its own spirit to receive a Spirit from above, to be one life, one love, one spirit with Christ in God. This prayer, which is an emptying itself of all its own lusts and natural tempers, and an opening itself for the light and love of God to enter into it, is the prayer in the Name of Christ, to which nothing is denied for the love which God bears to the soul. His eternal, never-ceasing desire to enter into it, to dwell in it, and open the birth of his Holy Word and Spirit in it stays no longer than till the door of the heart opens for him. For nothing does, or can keep God out of the soul, or hinder his holy union with it, but the desire of the heart turned from him. And the reason of it is this. It is because the life of the soul is in itself nothing else but a working will and therefore wherever the will works or goes, there, and there only, the soul lives, whether it be in God or the creature.

Nothing does or can go with us into Heaven. Nothing follows us into Hell, but that in which the will dwelt, with which it was fed, nourished and clothed in this life. And this is to be noted well, that death can make no alteration of this state of the will. It only takes off the outward, worldly covering of flesh and blood, and forces the soul to see and feel and know what a life, what a state, food, body and habitation, its own working will has brought forth in it.

Tell me, is there anything in life that deserves a thought, but how to keep this working of our will in a right state, and to get that purity of heart which alone can see and know and find and possess God? Is there anything so frightful as this worldly spirit which turns the soul from God, makes it a House of Darkness, and feeds it with the food of time at the expense of all the riches of eternity? On the other hand, what can be so desirable a good as the Spirit of Prayer, which empties the soul of all its own evil, separates death and darkness from it, leaves Self, time and the world, and becomes one life, one light, one love, one spirit with Christ and God and Heaven.

Think, my Friends, of these things with something more than thoughts. Let your hungry souls eat of the nourishment of them as a bread of Heaven, and desire only to live that with all the working of your wills and the whole spirit of your minds, you may live and die united to God.

Prayer is an opening to light and love.

Thursday of the Third Week of Lent

A reading on Christian charity from *A Serious Call to a Devout and Holy Life* by William Law.

Flavia and Miranda* are two maiden sisters, that have each of them an income of two hundred pounds a year. They buried their parents twenty years ago, and have since that time spent their estate as they pleased.

Flavia has been the wonder of all her friends, for her excellent management, in making so surprising a figure on so moderate a fortune. Several ladies that have twice her fortune are not able to be always so genteel, and so constant at all places of pleasure and expense. She has everything that is in the fashion, and is in every place where there is any diversion. Flavia is very orthodox, she talks warmly against heretics and schismatics, is generally at Church, and often at the Sacrament. She once commended a sermon that was against the pride and vanity of dress, and thought it was very just against Lucinda, whom she takes to be a great deal finer than she need to be. If any one asks Flavia to do something in charity, if she likes the person who makes the proposal, or happens to be in a right temper, she will toss him half-a-crown, or a crown, and tell him if he knew what a long milliner's bill she had just received, he would think it a great deal for her to give. When she hears a sermon upon the necessity of charity; she thinks the man preaches well, that it is a very proper subject, that people need very much to be reminded of it; but she applies nothing to herself, because she remembers that she gave a crown some time ago, when she could so ill spare it.

As for poor people themselves, she will admit of no complaints from them; she is very positive they are all cheats and liars, and will say anything to get relief; and therefore it must be a sin to encourage them in their evil ways.

Thus lives Flavia; and if she lives ten years longer she will have worn about two hundred different suits of clothes. Out of these thirty years of her life, fifteen will have been disposed of in bed; and, of the remaining fifteen, about fourteen will have been consumed in eating, drinking, dressing, visiting, conversation, reading and hearing plays and romances, at operas, assemblies, balls and diversions. For you may reckon all the time that she is up thus spent, except about an hour and a half that is disposed of at Church most Sundays in the year. With great management, and under mighty rules of economy, she will have spent six thousand pounds upon herself, leaving only some shillings, crowns, or half-crowns, that have gone from her in accidental charities.

I shall not take it upon me to say that it is impossible for Flavia to be saved; but thus much must be said, that she has no grounds from Scripture to think she is in the way of salvation. For her whole life is in direct opposition to all those practices which the Gospel commends for salvation.

And here it should be noticed well, that the poor, vain turn of mind, the irreligion, the folly, and vanity of this whole life of Flavia, is entirely owing to the manner of using her estate. It is this that has formed her spirit, that has given life to every idle temper, that has supported every trifling passion, and kept her from all thoughts of a prudent, useful, and devout life.

When her parents died, her only thought about her two hundred pounds a year was that she had so much money to do what she would with, to spend upon herself, and purchase the pleasures and gratifications of all her passions.

And it is this false judgment and indiscreet use of her fortune, that has filled her whole life with the same indiscretion, and kept her from thinking of what is right, and wise, and pious, in everything else.

She might have been humble, serious, devout, a lover of good books, an admirer of prayer and careful of her time, diligent in good works, full of charity and the love of God, but the imprudent use of her estate forced all the contrary tempers upon her. And it was no wonder that she should turn her time, her mind, her health, and strength, to the same uses as her fortune. It is owing to her being wrong in so great an article of life, that you can see nothing wise, or reasonable, or pious, in any other part of it.

The manner of using her estate has formed her spirit.

----

*Miranda is the subject of the meditation for the following Thursday.

Friday of the Third Week of Lent

A reading from a sermon by Charles Kingsley on the text: "I pray that you may have the power to comprehend, with all the saints, what is the breadth and length and height and depth, and to know the love of Christ that surpasses knowledge, so that you may be filled with all the fullness of God" (Ephesians 3:18–19).

The cross is our sign. It is God's everlasting token to us, that Christians are told something about God which none of the wisest among the heathen knew; which nothing but the cross can teach us.

There were those among the old heathens who believed in one God; and some of them saw that that God must be, on the whole, a good and a just God. But they could not help thinking of God (with very rare exceptions) as a respecter of persons, a God who had favorites; and at least, that God was one who loved friends and hated enemies, though the prophets in the Old Testament told a very different tale about God's love.

But that was all they could believe—in a God who was not unjust or wicked, but was at least hard, proud, unbending; while the notion that we could love our enemies, and bless those who used us despitefully and persecuted us—much less die for our enemies—that would have seemed impossible and absurd. They stumbled at the stumblingblock of the cross. God, they thought, would do to others as they did to God. If they loved God, God would love them. If they neglected God, God would hate and destroy them.

But when the apostles preached the Gospel, the good news of Christ crucified, they preached a very different tale; a tale quite new; utterly different from any that mankind had ever heard before.

And now do you take all this to be only ingenious fancies, and a pretty play of words? Ah, my friends, the day will come when you will find that the measure of Christ's cross is the most important question upon earth.

In the hour of death, and in the day of judgment; then the one thing which you will care to think of (if you can think at all then, as too many poor souls cannot, and therefore had best think of now before their wits fail them)—the one thing which you will care to think of, I say, will be—not, how clever you have been, how success-ful you have been, how much admired you have been, how much money you have made—"Of course not," you answer; "I shall be thinking of the state of my soul; whether I am fit to die; whether I have faith enough to meet God; whether I have good works enough to meet God."

Will you, my friend? Then you will soon grow tired of thinking of that likewise, at least I hope and trust that you will. For, however much faith you may have had, you will find that you have not had enough. However many good works you may have done, you will find that you have not done enough. The better person you are, the more you will be dissatisfied with yourself; the more you will be ashamed of yourself; till with all saints who have been worthy of the name of saints, you will be driven—if you are in earnest about your own soul—to give up thinking of yourself, and to think only of the cross of Christ, and of the love of Christ which shines thereon, and ask—Is it great enough to cover my sins? to save one as utterly unworthy to be saved as I? And so, after all, you will be forced to throw yourself where you ought to have thrown yourself at the onset—at the foot of Christ's cross; and say in spirit and in truth—

"Nothing in my hand I bring;

Simply to the cross, I cling."

In plain words, I throw myself, with all my sins, upon that absolute and boundless love of God which made all things, and me among them, and hates nothing that God has made, who redeemed all mankind, and me among them, and has said by the mouth of the only-begotten Son, "Anyone who comes to me I will never drive away."

Think only of the cross of Christ.

Saturday of the Third Week of Lent

A reading on baptism from two sermons by Frederick W. Robertson on the texts: "In Christ Jesus you are all children of God through faith. As many of you as were baptized into Christ have clothed yourselves with Christ. There is no longer Jew or Greek, there is no longer slave or free, there is no longer male and female; for all of you are one in Christ Jesus. And if you belong to Christ, then you are Abraham's offspring, heirs according to the promise" (Galatians 3:26–29). "Baptism, which this prefigured, now saves you—not as a removal of dirt from the body, but as an appeal to God for a good conscience, through the resurrection of Jesus Christ" (1 Peter 3:21).

Each human being is God's child, and the sin of humanity consists in perpetually living as if it were false. It is the sin of the heathen—and what is your mission to them but to tell them that they are God's children, and not living up to this privilege? But they were heirs already, if they only knew it. "Because you are children, God has sent the Spirit of his Son into our hearts, crying, 'Abba! Father!'" To be a child of God is one thing; to know that you are, and call God Father, is another—and that is regeneration.

Now, there was needed a permanent, and authoritative pledge, revealing and confirming this; for, to mankind in the mass, invisible truths become real only when they have been made visible. This pledge is baptism. Baptism takes the child and addresses it by name. Paul—no longer Saul—you are a child of God. Remember it from now on. *You*, Paul, are now regenerate: you will have foes to fight—the world, the flesh, and the devil—but remember, they only keep you out of an inheritance which is your own; not an inheritance which you have to win by some new feeling or merit in yourself. It *is* yours: you *are* the child of God; you *are* a member of Christ; you *are* an inheritor of the kingdom of heaven.

Notice, then, that baptism does not *create* a child of God. It does not make the fact; it only reveals it. If baptism made it a fact, then and there for the first time, baptism would be magic. No, faith does not create a child of God any more than baptism, nor does it make a fact. It only appropriates that which is a fact already.

The Catechism says: In baptism . . . I was *made* a child of God. Yes; coronation makes a Sovereign; but, paradoxical as it may seem, it can only *make* a sovereign one who is sovereign already. Crown a pretender, that coronation will not create the king. Coronation is the authoritative act of the nation declaring a fact which was fact before.

Similarly with baptism. Baptism makes a child of God in the sense in which coronation makes a king. And baptism naturally stands in Scripture for the title of regeneration and the moment of it. Only what coronation is in an earthly way, an authoritative manifestation of an invisible earthly truth, baptism is in a heavenly way—God's authoritative declaration in material form of spiritual reality. In other words, no bare sign, but a Divine Sacrament.

Let no one send you, with terrible self-inspection, to the dreadful task of searching your own soul for the warrant of your redemption, and deciding whether you have or not the feelings and the faith which give you a right to be one of God's elect. Better make up your mind at once you have not; you have no feelings that entitle you to that. Take your stand upon the broader, sublimer basis of God's Creation: God created the world; God redeemed the world. Baptism proclaims separately, personally, by name, to you, God created you—God redeemed you. Baptism is your warrant—you are God's child. And now, because you are God's child, live as a child of God; be redeemed from the life of evil, which is false to your nature, into the Life of Light and Goodness, which is the Truth of your Being. Scorn all that is mean; hate all that is false; struggle with all that is impure. Love "whatever is honorable, whatever is just, whatever is pure, whatever is pleasing, whatever is commendable," certain that God is on your side, and that whatever keeps you from God keeps you from your own Father. Live the simple, lofty life which befits an heir of immortality.

You are the child of God.

The Fourth Week of Lent

Love

Love bade me welcome: yet my soul drew back
    Guilty of dust and sin
But quick-eyed Love, observing me grow slack
    From my first entrance in,
Drew nearer to me sweetly questioning,
    If I lacked any thing.

A guest, I answered, worthy to be here:
    Love said, You shall be he.
I, the unkind, ungrateful? Ah my dear,
    I cannot look on thee.
Love took my hand, and smiling did reply,
    Who made the eyes but I?

Truth, Lord, but I have marred them; let my shame
    Go where it does deserve.
And know you not, says Love, who bore the blame?
    My dear, then I will serve.
You must sit down, says Love, and taste my meat:
    So I did sit and eat.

–George Herbert

The Fourth Sunday in Lent

A reading from *Footsteps of the Master* by
Harriet Beecher Stowe.

When a city is closely besieged and many of its outworks are destroyed, it is time to retreat to the citadel. In our day there is warm fighting about the outworks of Christianity. Many things are battered down that used to be thought indispensable to its defense. It is time to retreat to the citadel; and that citadel is Christ. Jesus Christ of Nazareth is still our King, our Light, our Law, our Leader. These names comprise all that a human being needs in this transitory, perplexing, and dangerous pilgrimage of life.

The Bible tells of a Being so One with the great Author of nature and the Source of all power that whoever has seen him has seen the Creator. It tells us that all things we behold in our material world were made by him and for him; that it has pleased the Father that in him should all fullness dwell, and that to him all things in heaven and on earth are made subject. It shows him to us from the beginning of time as constantly absorbed in the care and education of this world of ours. He has been the Desire of all nations—predicted, waited for, come at last!

And when he came and lived a mortal life what did he show the divine nature to be? It may all be told in one word: Love. Love, unconquered, unconquerable by human sin and waywardness. Love, sympathetic with the inevitable sorrows of human existence. Love, expressed in every form by which a God could express love. His touch was healing; the very hem of his garment had restoring virtue. He lived and loved as we live and love, only on a higher ideal—he gave to every human affection a more complete interpretation, a more perfect fullness. And finally, as the highest revelation of Love, he died for us, and in anguish and blood and dying pains still loved and prayed for us, the ungrateful human race. He passed through the night of death that he might learn not to fear it, and came forth radiant and immortal to tell us that we shall never die.

By a refinement of infinite mercy, the law of our lives is written not in hard statutes but in the life of this tender and sympathetic friend. Christ is our law. We learn courage, patience, fortitude, forgiving love from him. The lesson impossible in statute is made easy by sympathy. But lest the very brightness of the ideal fill us with despair we have his promise, "Lo, I am with you always to the end of the world! I will not leave you comfortless. I will come to you." Jesus, as an inseparable soul-friend—a consoler, a teacher, an enlightener—dwells on earth now in a higher sense than when he walked the hills of Palestine.

We hear much of modern skepticism. There is, perhaps, no more in the world now than there has always been, only its forms have changed. Its answer lies not in argument, but in the lives of Christ's followers. It was Christians who lived like Christ that won the first battle for Christianity, and it must be Christians who live like Christ that shall win the last. The life of faith in the Son of God, when fully lived out, always has been and always will be a victorious argument.

But to live this our faith must be firm. We cannot meet a skeptical world with weak faith. If we would draw our friend out of a swift-rushing current, our own feet must not stand on slippery places. We must seek faith in looking to him who has the giving of it. We must keep him before our minds and come so near him in daily prayer that we can say, "That which we have seen with our eyes, which we have looked upon and our hands have handled of the Word of Life, declare we unto you."

And even to those who have no conscious belief in Christ, his name can never be a matter of indifference. Whether they believe it or not, Christ stands to them in a peculiar relation that no other being holds. He is their best friend, the shepherd who is seeking them, the generous Savior and Giver of all that is longing to save them from all that they fear and to forgive exceeding abundantly beyond all they can ask or think.

Christ is our law.

Monday of the Fourth Week of Lent

A reading from a sermon by Mark Frank on the text: "Do you not know that in a race the runners all compete, but only one receives the prize? Run in such a way that you may win it" (1 Corinthians 9:24).

We must run this race in hope that through God's grace we may obtain the honor of heaven, the crown of glory: not fading and decaying pleasures, such as the leaves of the trees, or the flower of the field, that give a verdant beauty and fragrant smell for a while and vanish. Not for the praise of others are we to run our race, or do our works to be seen by them and be commended by them. "They," that do so, says Christ, "have their reward," but they have it and must look for no more; that is all they are likely to have. They have "beaten the air," and with the air they are passed away. Air they sought for, and air is all they have—a little foolish and vain breath, for all their pains. They can show nothing that they have obtained; and the very praise they sought proves nothing too; for not the one commended by others, "but . . . whom the Lord commends," is the only one truly praised and commended.

Heaven only it is we are to run to, and "Jesus, the author and finisher of our faith," our infinite and "exceeding great reward," and "the joy that was set before him," it is we are to look to; to no other recompense of reward, no other recompenser and rewarder.

To him now we are to look. If he himself set the joy of the right hand of the throne of God before his eyes, that he might the better "endure the cross," and "despise the shame," and "so run the race" that his Father set him, if he had an eye to the recompense of reward, then certainly we may set such a consideration before us, and they talk they know not what that deny it. God allures us by rewards, and Christ himself preaching the Gospel began it with this encouragement to incite us to listen to it, because "the kingdom of heaven" was "at hand." Set we then those joys before us, and fear not; look we, in all our tribulations and sufferings, upon them, to comfort and uphold us, in all our difficulties to encourage us, in all our devotions to inflame us. We consider that all we do, all we suffer, is nothing to be compared to the "crown of glory" that is "laid up" for us; that all our pains and labor, going and running and sweating and blowing for Christ, is not to be mentioned or thought upon, so that at last we may "obtain."

Yet to keep our spirits in awe, and keep down the pride that is likely to arise sometimes upon our well running and to make us diligent and constant in our course, let us remember, it is but a "may obtain"; we may miss as well, and shall too, if we run not orderly or give out. It is no more than "we shall reap, if we faint not." If we fail or faint, we shall not, our kingdom is removed, our crown is gone. "Work" we then our "salvation out with fear and trembling," as the Apostle advises us. It is common, but it is the greatest vanity and fallacy in the world, to think to get to heaven without pains, to go thither with all kinds of pomp, and ease, and pleasures. It is no such thing; the way is strait and narrow that leads there, says he who came to show it; and a race here we have to run for it, and all the way but a "may," a possibility or a probability, not a necessity to obtain it. We look carefully to our feet, apply ourselves diligently to our course, to run the ways of righteousness and peace, of holiness and salvation. Let us often look up to heaven and the "crown of glory laid up" there to add wings and spirit to us; and let us also look down sometimes to the dangers by the way, and mark our steps lest we chance to stumble and fall, to grow faint or weary; but that we may run lawfully, carefully, speedily, cheerfully, stoutly, patiently, and constantly to the end; that so running, we may obtain the end of our hopes: the crown of our joy, the salvation of our souls, and the redemption of our bodies, everlasting life, and eternal glory.

Run patiently and constantly.

Tuesday of the Fourth Week of Lent

From a sermon by Phillips Brooks on the text: "And whenever you fast, do not look dismal, like the hypocrites, for they disfigure their faces so as to show others that they are fasting. Truly I tell you, they have received their reward. But when you fast, put oil on your head and wash your face, so that your fasting may be seen not by others but by your Father who is in secret; and your Father who sees in secret will reward you"(Matthew 6:16–18).

This is the philosophy of fasting. It expresses repentance, and it uncovers the life to God. "Come down, my pride; stand back my passions; for I am wicked, and I wait for God to bless me." That is what the fasting individual says. You see what I mean by fasting. It is the voluntary disuse of anything innocent in itself, with a view to spiritual culture. It does not apply to food alone. It applies to everything which we may desire. We may fast from costliness of dress, from sumptuous houses, from exhilarating company, from music, from art, considered as sensuous delights. There are times when some deep experience, some profound humility of repentance, rejects them all. Not they but their opposites become the soul's true utterance. In its sorrow for its sins, all sumptuousness jars upon it. The feast and the feast's music are out of place. By emptiness and not by fullness that self-contempt, that sense of the vanity of the spirit's search to find goodness in itself must be expressed.

Now let us think about the value of fasting as a symbol. It expresses the abandonment of pride. But it is the characteristic of a symbolic action that it not merely expresses but increases and nourishes the feeling to which it corresponds. Laughter is the symbol of joy, but as you laugh your laughter reacts upon the joy and heightens it. Tears are the sign of sorrow, but they feed themselves the sorrow out of which they grow. Cheers are the expression of enthusiasm, but as the crowd sends up its shouts its zeal deepens and glows the brighter. And so if abstinence is the sign of humility, it is natural enough that as the life abstains from its ordinary indulgences, the humiliation which is repentance, should be deepened by its expression. Thus the symbol becomes also a means.

The question is not whether indulgence is wicked, whether God will punish you for doing certain things. The question is whether that thing is keeping other better things away from you; whether behind its little hulk the vast privilege and dignity of duty is hid from you; whether it stands between God and your soul. If it does, then it is an offence to you, and though it be your right hand or your right eye, cut it off, pluck it out, and cast it from you. The advantage and joy will be not in its absence, for you will miss it very sorely, but in what its loss reveals, in the new life which lies beyond it, which you will see stretching out and tempting you as soon as it is gone. To put aside everything that hinders the highest from coming to us, and then to call to us that highest which, no, Who is always waiting to come. Fasting and prayer—this, as the habit and tenor of a life, is noble. As an occasional effort even, if it is real and earnest, it makes the soul freer for the future. A short special communion with the unseen and eternal prevents the soul from ever being again so completely the slave of the things of sense and time.

Come down, my pride.

Wednesday of the Fourth Week of Lent

A reading on prayer from *The Book of Private Devotion* by Hannah More.

In prayer, the perfections of God, and especially God's mercies in our redemption, should occupy our thoughts as much as our sins; our obligations to God as much as our departures from God. We should keep up in our hearts a constant sense of our own weakness, not with a design to discourage the mind and depress the spirits, but with a view to drive us out of ourselves in search of the divine assistance. We should contemplate our infirmity in order to draw us to look to God for strength and to seek that power from God which we vainly look for in ourselves. We do not tell a sick friend of danger in order to grieve and terrify our friend, but to induce the friend to apply to the physician, and to have recourse to the remedy.

The success of prayer, though promised to all who offer it in perfect sincerity, is not so frequently promised to the cry of distress, to the impulse of fear, or the emergency of the moment, as to humble perseverance in devotion. It is to patient waiting, to assiduous solicitation, to unwearied importunity, that God has promised to lend an ear, to give the communication of the spirit, to grant the return of our requests. Nothing but this holy perseverance can keep up in our minds a humble sense of our dependence. It is not by a more casual petition, however passionate, but by habitual application, that devout affections are stimulated and maintained, that our converse with heaven is carried on. It is by no other means that we can be assured with St. Paul that "We are risen with Christ," but this obvious one—that we seek the things that are above—that the heart is renovated, that the mind is lifted above this low scene of things, that the Spirit breathes in a purer atmosphere, that the whole person is enlightened and strengthened and purified. And all this results the more frequently, and so the more nearly, as we approach the throne of God.

Through Jesus alone we have access with boldness to the throne of grace. He is our advocate with the Father. When the believer appears before God in secret, the Savior appears also, for "he always lives to make intercession for us." He has not only directed us to call upon the Father as "Our Father," and ask God to supply our daily needs, and forgive us our trespasses, but has graciously assured us that he "will do whatever you ask in his name, so that the Father may be glorified in the Son." All need for blessings suited to our various situations and circumstances in this mortal life, all that will be necessary for us in the power of death, and all that can minister to our happiness in a world of glory, God has graciously promised, and given us a command to ask for, in his name. And what is this but to plead, when praying to our heavenly Father, that Jesus has sent us, and to ask and expect the blessings for his sake alone?

God is faithful who has promised. God says, "Those who love me, I will deliver; I will protect those who know my name. When they call to me, I will answer them; I will be with them in trouble, I will rescue them and honor them" (Psalm 91:14, 15). God's promises are evidently designed to direct us in our supplications and to arouse in us an expectation of their fulfillment. And what is prayer but the offering of the desires of the heart for some good thing, which the Lord has directly or indirectly promised in God's holy word to bestow? The very act itself implies the blessing may be granted in answer to our petitions; and God's promises assure us it will, though the time and manner of conferring it are reserved to God, God best knows what will suit us, and the best possible time for bestowing it. Therefore the one who obeys the divine precepts heartily pleads the promises in prayer perseveringly, waits their fulfillment patiently, and is content if God is glorified, though the self be not gratified and may confidently expect seasonable and suitable answers to all the prayers offered in sincerity at the throne of grace in the name of Jesus.

God answers patient waiting.

Thursday of the Fourth Week of Lent

※◇※

A reading on Christian charity from *A Serious Call to a Devout and Holy Life* by William Law.

Miranda (the sister of Flavia) is a sober, reasonable Christian: as soon as she was mistress of her time and fortune, it was her first thought how she might best fulfil everything that God required of her in the use of them, and how she might make the best and happiest use of this short life. She depends upon the truth of what our blessed Lord has said, that there is but "One thing needful," and therefore makes her whole life but one continual labor after it. She has but one reason for doing or not doing, for liking or not liking anything, and that is, the will of God. She is not so weak as to pretend to add what is called the fine lady to the true Christian; Miranda thinks too well to be taken with the sound of such silly words; she has renounced the world to follow Christ in the exercise of humility, charity, devotion, abstinence, and heavenly affections.

Miranda does not divide her duty between God, her neighbor, and herself; but she considers all as due to God, and so does everything in God's Name, and for God's sake. This makes her consider her fortune as the gift of God, that is to be used, as everything is that belongs to God, for the wise and reasonable ends of a Christian and holy life. Her fortune therefore is divided between herself and several other poor people, and she has only her part of relief from it. She thinks it the same folly to indulge herself in needless, vain expenses, as to give to other people to spend in the same way. Therefore as she will not give a poor man money to go see a puppet-show, neither will she allow herself any to spend in the same manner; thinking it very proper to be as wise herself as she expects poor men should be. For it is a folly and a crime in a poor man, says Miranda, to waste what is given him in foolish trifles, while he wants meat, drink, and clothes.

It may be, says Miranda, that I may often give to those that do not deserve it, or that will make an ill use of my alms. But what then? Is not this the very method of Divine goodness? Does not God make his "sun to rise on the evil and on the good"? Is not this the very goodness that is recommended to us in Scripture, that, by imitating of it, we may be children of our Father in Heaven, who "sends rain on the just and on the unjust"? And shall I withhold a little money, or food, from my fellow-creatures, for fear they should not be good enough to receive it of me? Do I beg of God to deal with me, not according to my merit, but according to God's own great goodness; and shall I be so absurd as to withhold my charity from a poor brother or sister, because they may perhaps not deserve it? Shall I use a measure towards them, which I pray God never to use towards me?

You will perhaps say, that by this means I encourage people to be beggars. But the same thoughtless objection may be made against all kinds of charities, for they may encourage people to depend upon them. The same may be said against clothing the naked, or giving medicines to the sick; for that may encourage people to neglect themselves, and be careless of their health. But when the love of God dwells in you, when it has enlarged your heart, and filled you with bowels of mercy and compassion, you will make no more such objections as these.

This is the spirit, and this is the life, of the devout Miranda; and if she lives ten years longer, she will have spent sixty hundred pounds in charity, for that which she allows herself, may fairly be reckoned amongst her alms.

When she dies, she must shine among Apostles, and saints, and martyrs; she must stand among the first servants of God, and be glorious among those that have fought the good fight, and finished their course with joy.

She considers all as due to God.

Friday of the Fourth Week of Lent

A reading from "An Exhortation to the Carrying of Christ's Cross" by Myles Coverdale.

You are of those who have made a covenant with God to forsake themselves and Satan in this world. You are of those who have their loins girded about, and their lights burning in their hands, like men and women who wait for their Lord's coming. You are of those who will worship the Lord God only, and will not worship the works of human hands, though the oven burn never so hot. You are in the number of them to whom Christ is precious and dear.

Therefore, dearly beloved, remember that your joy and paradise is not here, your companions are not the multitude of worldlings, and such as seek to please others and to live here at ease in the service of Satan. But you are of another world: Christ is your captain; your joy is in heaven, your companions are the patriarchs, prophets, apostles, martyrs, confessors, and the dear saints of God who followed the Lamb wherever he went, knowing this life and world to be full of evil, a warfare, a smoke, a shadow, a vapor, replenished and environed with all kind of miseries.

You ought not to think it any strange thing, if misery, trouble, adversity, persecution, and displeasure come upon you. For how can it be otherwise? Can the world love you, who are not its own? Worldly people are the soldiers of your chief enemy, and can they regard you? Can Satan permit you to rest, if you will not do him homage? Will you expect to travel, and have no foul way nor rain? Will shipmen shrink, or sailors of the sea, if storms arise? Do they not look for such? And, dearly beloved, did we not enter into God's ship and ark of baptism at the first? Will you then count it strange, if perils and tempests blow? Are you not traveling to your heavenly city of Jerusalem, where all is joy and felicity, and will you now tarry by the way for storms or showers? The market and fair will then be past; the door will be barred, and the bride will be at supper. Therefore away with dainty niceness. Will you think the Father of heaven will deal more gently with you in this age, than God has done with other dearest friends in other ages? What way and weather, what storms and tempests, what disease, trouble, and disquietness found all the apostles and evangelists: yes, of Jesus Christ our Lord, the dear Son and darling of God! How many and great are the martyrs, confessors, and those who shed their blood in this life rather than be stained in their journey, or lodge in any of Satan's inns: so that the storms or winds which fell in their travelings might not touch them.

Why then are we so fearful, unwilling, and backward to leave that which, will we, nill we, we must leave, and that so shortly, that we know not the time when? Where is our renouncing and forsaking of the world and the flesh, which we solemnly swore in baptism? Ah, shameless cowards that we are who will not follow the track of so many patriarchs, kings, priests, prophets, apostles, evangelists, and saints of God, yes, even of the very Son of God! How many now go with you, as I and all your friends in bonds and exile for the gospel? You shall see in us, that we preached no lies nor tales of tubs; but even the very true word of God, for which we, by God's grace and help of your prayers, willingly and joyfully give our blood to be shed, as already we have given liberally our goods, living friends, and natural country. For now we are certain that we are on the highway to heaven's bliss; as Paul says, "By many tribulations and persecutions we must enter into God's kingdom." And because we would go thither ourselves, and bring you thither also, therefore the devil stirs up the coals. And forasmuch as we all loitered in the way, he therefore has received power of God to overcast the weather and to stir up storms, that we, God's children, might go faster. Therefore, like God's children, let us go on forward apace; the wind is on our back, hoist up the sails, lift up your hearts and hands unto God in prayer, and keep your anchor of faith to cast in time on the rock of God's word, and on his mercy in Christ.

Lift up your heart.

Saturday of the Fourth Week of Lent

A reading from a sermon on baptism by Frederick W. Robertson on the text: "In Christ Jesus you are all children of God through faith. As many of you as were baptized into Christ have clothed yourselves with Christ. There is no longer Jew or Greek, there is no longer slave or free, there is no longer male and female; for all of you are one in Christ Jesus. And if you belong to Christ, then you are Abraham's offspring, heirs according to the promise" (Galatians 3:26–29).

Notice these two blessings of a true understanding of baptism: First, it prevents exclusiveness and spiritual pride, and all condemnation and contempt of others because it admits those who have no spiritual capacity or consciousness to be God's children. It proclaims a kingdom, not for a few favorites, but for all mankind. It protests against the idea that God's relationship to us depends on feelings. It asserts it as a broad, grand, universal, blessed fact. It bids you pray with a meaning of added majesty in the words, *Our* Father.

Take care. Do not say of others that they are unregenerate. Do not make a distinction within the church of Christians and not-Christians. If you do, what do you more than the Pharisees of old? That wretched beggar that holds his hat at the crossing of the street is God's child as well as you, if he only knew it. You know it—he does not; that is the difference; but the immortal is in him too, and the Eternal Word speaks in him. That daughter of dissipation whom you despise, spending night after night in frivolity, she, too, has a Father in Heaven. "My Father and *your* Father, my God and *your* God." She has forgotten him, and, like the prodigal, is trying to live on the husks of the world—the empty husks which will not satisfy—the degrading husks which the swine did eat. But, whether she will or not, her baptism is valid, and proclaims a fact—which may be, alas! the worse for her, if she will not have it the better.

Second, baptism proclaims a church—humanity joined in Christ, to God. We are not merely a collection of atoms, a sand heap piled together with no cohesion among ourselves, or a mass of steel-filings cleaving separately to a magnet, but not to each other. Do not say that, because the church is separated from the world, therefore the world are not God's children. Rather that very separation proves it. You baptize a separate body in order to realize that which is true of the collective race, as in this text—"There is neither Jew nor Greek." In all things it is the same. If you would sanctify all time, you set apart a sabbath—not to show that other days are not intended to be sacred, but for the very purpose of making them sacred. If you would have a "nation of priests," you set apart a priesthood; not as if the priestly functions were exclusively in that body, but in order, by concentration, to bring out to greater perfection the priestly character which is shared by the whole, and then thereby make the whole more truly "priests to God to offer spiritual sacrifices." In the same way, if God would baptize humanity, God baptizes a separate church, in order that that church may baptize the race. The church is God's ideal of humanity realized.

And third, this doctrine of baptism sanctifies materialism. The things of earth are pledges and sacraments of things in heaven. It is not for nothing that God has selected for sacraments the commonest of all acts—a meal—and the most abundant of all materials—water. Do you think that God means to say that only through two channels the Spirit streams into the soul? Or is it not much more in unison with God's dealings to say, that these two are set apart to signify to us the sacramental character of all nature?—just as a miracle was intended not to reveal God working there, at that death-bed and in that storm, but to call attention to God's presence in every death and every storm. Go out at this spring season of the year, see the mighty preparations for life that Nature is making, feel the swelling sense of gratefulness, and the pervasive expanding consciousness of love for all Being, and then say whether this whole Form, which we call Nature, is not the great Sacrament of God, the revelation of God's existence, and the channel of God's communications to the spirit!

You are all children of God.

The Fifth Week of Lent

Holy Sonnets – 13

You have made me, and shall your work decay?
Repair me now, for now my end does haste;
I run toward death and death meets me as fast,
And all my pleasures are like yesterday.
I dare not move my dim eyes any way;
Despair behind and death before do cast
Such terror, and my feeble flesh does waste
By sin in it, which it towards hell does weigh.
Only you are above, and when I gaze
By your leave toward your throne, I rise again.
But our old subtle foe so tests my days
That not one hour my self I can sustain.
Your Grace may wing me to prevent his art,
And you like Adamant draw my iron heart.

–John Donne

The Fifth Sunday in Lent

A reading from *The Incarnation of the Son of God* by
Charles Gore.

We learn from the incarnation that the quality of the divine personality is love. The thought of the fatherhood of God, in that moral sense which implies his love, is so familiar, at least superficially, to us, that the less thoughtful among us are apt to assume it as something self-evident; as if it were a matter of course apart from Christ's revelation. But it does not require much thought to enable us to perceive, or much bitter experience or much sympathy to enable us to feel, that the world apart from Christ gives us no adequate assurance that God is Love. The psalmist indeed argues, "He that made the eye, shall he not see?" and Robert Browning has taught us to add: "He that created love, shall He not love?"

But, if love in human beings indicates love in God, whose offspring we are, yet there is much on the other hand to give us pause in drawing such a conclusion. Not only the inexorable, remorseless aspect of physical nature seems against it, but also the fact that love even in humanity, as we contemplate it "writ large" in history, appears often feeble and helpless by the side of human lust and bitterness and cruelty and selfishness and untrustworthiness.

That God is love means, of course, not merely that there exists such a thing as love in the world, nor merely that it represents something in God. It carries with it also the assurance that love is the motive of creation, and the realization of the purpose of love its certain goal: that love exists in that supreme perfection in which the universality of its range over all creatures diminishes nothing from its particular application to each individual. That love is God's motive;

that love is victorious; that love is universal in range and unerringly individual in application, in a word that *God is love*—it is this that our Lord guarantees, because *he* has translated divine love into the intelligible lineaments of the corresponding human quality. We behold in Jesus' love the motive, love individualizing, love impartial and universal, love victorious through death; and the one who has seen him, we know has seen the Father; his love is the Father's love; there is nothing behind it to overcome it, nothing outside it to escape it, nothing below it to be too small for it. This is the Christian Gospel.

We must observe that this revelation of the love of God is not like a scientific discovery, which once made and published is independent of its originator, and would be in no way affected if his personality were to fade into darkness or oblivion. For Jesus Christ did not satisfy our minds with arguments, he did not solve objections, or show us why pain and sacrifice are necessary throughout creation; no, he did not even declare God's love as a dogma and prove it by miracles. The gospel lies in his person. He took upon himself all that tells against divine love, all that has ever wrung from human hearts the bitter words of unbelief, or the more chastened cry of agonizing inquiry, "My God, my God, why have you forsaken me?" He took all this upon himself, and as the man of sorrows, made it, in his bitter passion and death upon the cross, the very occasion for expressing the depth of the divine self-sacrifice. Thus the satisfaction that he gives us lies in his proving to us, out of the very heart of all that might seem to speak against such a conclusion, that behind all the groaning and travailing of creation lies the love of God, and beyond it all the victory of God; and the demonstration consists in the fact that Jesus as essential Son of the Father reveals no other love than God's, and by his resurrection from the dead manifests that love triumphant through all seeming failure.

Behind all the travail lies the love of God.

Monday of the Fifth Week of Lent

A reading on discipline from a sermon by John Keble on the theme of "Christ's Preparation for his Passion."

Is there anyone who does not know people who think little of public worship because experience tells them, as they suppose, that one may be good and useful without it? And can it be reasonably doubted that many go on to despise private prayer also, because they do not see why it should be necessary to people doing their duty to their acquaintance, and being useful in their generation? Now I do not say it is so bad, yet it may be a part of this same indevout temper, to despise and neglect, I say willfully to despise and neglect, any ordinance of the Church, any sort of direct devotion, which she recommends to her children. Fasting, for example, is one sort of private devotion on which the Church has given very particular directions, as any one may see in the calendar at the beginning of the Prayer Book. Yet how many persons are there, who pass by these directions altogether, making no difference at all between fast-days and feast-days! No doubt, most people do so in ignorance; their attention has never been really drawn to the subject: but whoever first began this inattention, whoever, being reminded, still goes on in it, have we not some reason to fear that it may be in them a symptom of the profane spirit of the world, to which all days and all times are alike? What would such a one have said to our Lord's devotions, that last week of his life, by night in the Mount of Olives? Would he not have thought it a pity, that working so hard as he did, and having so much to endure, he should weary himself still more with watching and prayer all night? But we see that he, to whom only the right way is perfectly known, took the way of self-denial and holy contemplation; he added watching and devotional exercises, by night and when alone, to the pastoral and charitable works, which engaged him by day.

Add to this the reflection, who our Blessed Lord was: God Incarnate; so united, even as a human being to the most high and eternal Godhead, that he could not be for a moment left alone. Yet even he accounted it necessary, at set times and places, and in a solemn manner, to keep up this intercourse of devotion with his heavenly Father. He who of all people, one should think, could least need it, has set the strictest example of intense prayer and retired meditation as the true way of preparing oneself for hard duties and conflicts in life and for the last unknown hour.

I wish we thought of this more than we do. Here is our Master rising up to his prayers a great while before day, and we lie on in sloth and negligence. Here is our Master on the Mount of Olives, after a hard day's work in the temple, and we, perhaps, fancying ourselves over-tired, come in and throw ourselves on our beds without one serious prayer or recollection. Here is our Master kneeling and falling prostrate, and we sit carelessly, and perhaps look about us, while the Church is offering up the most solemn prayers.

You are deceived, my friends, if you imagine that these are mere outward things, making no difference, if the heart be right. Why are they set down as part of our Lord's behavior, if they make no difference in God's sight? How can they be mere outward things, if we do them humbly because we read that he did so? If place, posture, time, self-denial, helped him in his devotions; are we better than he (God forgive the word), that we should think ourselves above needing such help?

Be not, then, slothful, in this holy and blessed season; make haste to be reconciled, you who are out of charity; deny yourselves, you who live at your ease; recollect yourselves, you who are careless in your prayers; and remember your Savior, while you have time.

Outward things make a difference.

Tuesday of the Fifth Week of Lent

A reading on fasting from a sermon by Lancelot Andrewes preached before King James I on Ash Wednesday, 1619, on the text: "Yet even now, says the LORD, return to me with all your heart, with fasting, with weeping, and with mourning; rend your hearts and not your clothing. Return to the LORD, your God" (Joel 2:12–13).

We must turn, with the heart, with the whole heart. Is this all? No, we must turn "with fasting." Take heed of turning "with" into "without." We may not turn without fasting. We must also turn back our eye and reflect on our past sins, be sorry for them, before our turning will be as it should.

I know we would like to have the sentence end here, have the matter between our hearts and us, and end it there with no more ado. But the Prophet tells us that our repentance is to be incorporated into the body no less than the sin was. Hers has been the delight of sin, and she too must bear a part of the penalty, so that the heart within and the body without may both turn since both have gone astray. It is a tax, a tribute, it has pleased God to lay on our sins, and we must bear it.

What strange ideas are abroad in the world on this point. Flesh and blood reveals a far more easy way, not encumbered with any of these. To "turn" and yet not lose a meal all the year long, and not shed a tear, and not rend a garment, and yet do very well. And with this idea they pass their lives, and with this they pass out of their lives, resolved, as it seems to gamble with their souls and to come to heaven after their own fashion or not come there at all.

Now, would they, being ready to return, make a feast the same day they are to do it with light, merry hearts and cheerful looks and not, instead, with shame in their countenance, fear in their hearts, grief in their eyes?

The Church makes this time of our return a time of fasting and prescribed it not only by way of prescription to keep the body low, that it may be a less fertile soil for the sins of the flesh, but awards it as a chastisement for sins past. For to be restricted from that which otherwise we might freely use has the nature of a punishment. The psalm says, "I chastened myself with fasting," so it is a chastisement.

And thus we preach fasting: 1. Not as the Physicians enjoin it in their wisdom, to digest some former surfeit; 2. Nor as the Philosophers in their morals, to keep the senses responsive; 3. Nor as the government in their proclamations to preserve the breed of cattle or increase strength by sea; but as the holy Prophets of God do we prescribe it, and to a religious end: even to chasten ourselves for sin by this forbearance. So no physical, philosophical, political fast, but a prophetical, yes an evangelical fast. For if in sorrow we are to fast when "the bridegroom is taken away," much more when we ourselves, by our sins committed, have been the cause of his taking, indeed of his driving away from us.

And must we then fast? Indeed we must, or get a new Epistle for the day, and a new Gospel too. For as God in the Epistle commands it, so Christ in the Gospel presupposes it, taking it for granted that we will fast. So surely fast we must, or else tell God and Christ that they are not well advised; we have found a way beyond them, to turn to God without any fasting at all.

It is not the decay of nature but the chastisement of sin the Church seeks. But at this door we all escape: we are all weak and crazy when we would repent, but lusty and strong when it comes to committing sin. Our physicians will easily tell us and we will easily believe any that will tell us "favor yourselves; it is not for you." Take heed; "God is not mocked." God, who would have sin chastened, sees, I fear, that the pleasing of our appetite is the true cause and the endangering of our health but a pretense, and God will not have God's laws thus dallied with, fast or loose. "Turn to God with fasting" or be ready to show a good cause why, and to show it to God. It is God who calls for it, and God knows best what turning will serve our turn.

Turn with fasting.

Wednesday of the Fifth Week of Lent

A reading from a sermon on prayer by Phillips Brooks on the text: "If you abide in me, and my words abide in you, ask for whatever you wish, and it will be done for you" (John 15:7).

In one shape or another the religious question which gives thoughtful, religious people the most trouble is probably the question of Prayer. We cannot doubt that it has always been so. We feel sure that in every condition of religion, down to the lowest, in which human beings are moved to supplicate God at all, the struggle between the two feelings, between the instinct that God must hear and answer, and the doubt whether God can hear and answer, has been always going on. It is not a struggle of our days alone; it is not a question which certain peculiar tendencies of our time have brought out.

Is it possible for the great First Cause to be laid open to appeals which originate in human wills, and so to yield to causes behind God in governing God's action? You see our very jealousness for God's honor comes and lays itself across the path by which our timid souls are creeping to the mercy-seat. The very greatness which tempts us to trust God seems to forbid us to ask.

"If ye abide in me." Oh, my dear friends, how many of our prayers must go unprayed, if we sent them up to the mercy-seat through that judgment-chamber where the words of Jesus sit! How many times we have complained that our prayer brought no answer, when it was a prayer we never could have prayed unless we first drove out every word of Christ from its abiding-place within us! Is there a Christian here who can declare before God that he or she ever prayed to God in perfect submission to Christ's will, in perfect conformity to Christ's

Words, and got no answer? Not here; not in all the world; not in all the ages!

This is the meaning of Christ's promise: The true Christian must always have an answer to prayer, because we can never pray a prayer incapable of answer. Does it sound like a mere truism? Is it an insignificant conclusion that we have reached? Does it amount to nothing to say that Christ will grant all our prayers because we cannot ask anything that God is not willing and anxious to grant already? Surely there is no weakening of the thought of prayer in this. How would you strengthen it? Would you say that the good Christian may ask of God things that God is unwilling to bestow, and gain them? But why is God unwilling to bestow them except for one of two causes: either that the giving of them would injure the soul that asks them, or that it would interfere with some plan that the divine wisdom has shaped for the universe at large? In either case can you conceive of a true and filial prayer demanding the unwilling boon? Grant that Christians have the power, will they use it? Must they not in using it depart out of that harmony with Christ which is the very condition of success, cease to abide in him, and so fail of the dangerous gift that is desired?

The result of our whole study of Prayer today seems to be this, that it involves far more than we ordinarily think—a certain necessary relation between the soul and God. The condition of prayer is personal; it looks to character. How this rebukes our ordinary slipshod notions of what it is to pray! God's mercy-seat is no mere stall set by the vulgar roadside, where every careless passer-by may put an easy hand out to snatch any glittering blessing that catches the eye. It stands in the holiest of holies. We can come to it only through veils and by altars of purification. To enter into it, we must enter into God.

All prayer must be answered.

Thursday of the Fifth Week of Lent

A reading on charity from a sermon by Henry Smith entitled "The Poor Man's Tears" on the text: "whoever gives even a cup of cold water to one of these little ones in the name of a disciple—truly I tell you, none of these will lose their reward" (Matthew 10:42).

Alms is a charitable relief given by the godly to the sick, the lame, the blind, the impotent, the needy, the hungry and poorest persons, all those who are daily vexed with want, to whom even in duty, and not compassion, we ought to give some part of that which God has mercifully bestowed on us. For as we daily seek for benefits at God's hand, which God does continually give us, so we should use it to relieve the poor. The performance of this we ought not to put off from time to time, but to do it when they desire to have it done. For true obedience to God forbids us to prolong or put off the doing of good things.

O let us take heed that our hearts are not hardened against the poor nor that we give our alms to get glory from the world, but so let us give our alms that the one hand may not know what the other does. Yes, we ought to give with such equality that our poor neighbors may be relieved. It is a good society that looks to every member in the society, and those people are worthy of riches who look daily to the feeding of their poor neighbors.

Let therefore the tears of the poor admonish you to charity, that when Dives has dined Lazarus may have the crumbs.

As to how much we should give, we are taught that if we have much we should give accordingly, if we have but little, give what we can spare. Saint Luke counseled us, if we have two coats we must give one to him that hath none; and of meat likewise. But as touching this question little needs to be spoken when our own covetous hearts are ready enough to frame excuses.

Some will say they do not know the party that demanded relief or begs alms of them. Oh! say some, I suspect he is an idle person, dishonest, or perhaps not thrifty, and therefore refuse to give any relief at all. To this I answer, they are needless doubts, for we ought to relieve them, if we do not know them to be such persons, and let their bad deeds fall on their own necks, for if they perish for want we are in danger of God's wrath. We are not tied to one place for giving our charity, but it stretches far; we are commanded not only to relieve our own countrymen, but also strangers and such as dwell in foreign nations.

The tears of men, women, and children are grievous and pitiful; and tears give cause of great compassion, especially the tears of those who are constrained to beg for their relief. But if the tears of the rich for the loss of their goods, or the tears of parents for the death of their children, or the tears of kind-natured persons for the loss of friends, or other wrongs sustained ought generally to be regarded and pitied, then much more should the tears of those breed great compassion in the hearts of Christians whom beggary and extremity of miserable hunger produce tears of the most grievous and lamentable sort. Oh, what shall we say to those pitiful faces which are made moist through the extremity of hunger, in which are most bitter and sharp effects, a thing above all extremes?

Tears are the last thing that man, woman, or child can move by, and where tears move not, nothing will move. I therefore exhort you, by the lamentable tears which the poor do daily shed through hunger and extreme misery, to be good to them, to be charitable and merciful to them, and to relieve those whom you see with misery distressed.

The Scripture says, Give to every one who asks. God gave herbs and other food to every living thing. Every society that lets any member of it perish for hunger is an unnatural and uncharitable society. But people are nowadays so full of doubts, through a covetous desire for themselves, that they cannot abide to part with anything for the poor, in spite of the fact that God has promised not to forget the work and love which you have showed to the poor and distressed.

Let the tears of the poor admonish you to charity.

Friday of the Fifth Week of Lent

A meditation on the cross from *Poems, Centuries, and Three Thanksgivings* by Thomas Traherne.

Lord Jesus, what love shall I render to you, for your love to me, your eternal love! Oh what fervor, what ardor, what humiliation, what reverence, what joy, what adoration, what zeal, what thanksgiving! You are perfect in beauty, you are the king of eternal glory, you reign in the highest heavens and yet came down from heaven to die for me! And shall not I live for you? O my joy! O my sovereign friend! O my life and my all! I beseech you to let those trickling drops of blood that run down your flesh drop upon me. O let your love inflame me: love so deep and infinite that you suffered the wrath of God for me, and purchased all nations and kingdoms to be my treasures; you redeemed me from hell, and when you had overcome the sharpness of death you opened the kingdom of heaven to all believers; What shall I do for you?

What shall I do for you, O preserver of all: live, love, and admire; and learn to become such to you as you are to me. O glorious soul, whose comprehensive understanding at once contains all kingdoms and ages! O glorious mind, whose love extends to all creatures! O miraculous and eternal God-head, now suffering on the cross for me:

Why, Lord Jesus, do you love us, why are we your treasures? What wonder is this, that you should esteem us so as to die for us? Show me the reasons of your love that I may love all others too. O goodness ineffable! they are the treasures of your goodness who so infinitely love them that you gave yourself for them. Your goodness delighted to be communicated to them whom you had saved. O you who are most glorious in goodness, make me abundant in this goodness like yourself, that I may as deeply pity others' misery, and as ardently thirst for their happiness as you do. Let the same mind be in me that is in Christ Jesus, for those who are not led by the Spirit of Christ are none of his. Holy Jesus, I admire your love; I admire your love to me also. O that I could see it through all those wounds! O that I could feel it in all those stripes! O that I could hear it in all those groans! O that I could taste it beneath that gall and vinegar! O that I could smell the savor of thy sweet ointments, even in this Golgotha or Place of a Skull. I pray you to teach me first your love to me, and then to all mankind! But in your love to mankind I am beloved.

These wounds are in themselves openings too small to let in my sight to the vast comprehension of your eternal love. These wounds engraved in your hands are only shady impressions; unless I see the glory of your soul, in which the fulness of the God-head dwells bodily. These bloody characters are too dim to let me read it, in its luster and perfection till I see your person and know your ways! O you that hang upon this cross before my eyes, whose face is bleeding and covered over with tears and filth and blows! Angels adore the glory of your Godhead in the highest heavens who in every thought, and in every work did glorious things for me from everlasting! What could I, O my Lord, desire more than such a world! Such heavens and such an earth, such beasts and fowls and fishes made for me! All these do homage to me, and I have dominion over them from the beginning! The heavens and the earth minister to me, as if no one were created but I alone. I willingly acknowledge it to be your gift, your bounty to me! How many thousand ways do others also minister to me! O what riches have you prepared out of nothing for me! All creatures labor for my sake, and I am made to enjoy all your creatures. O what praises shall I return to you, the wisdom of the Creator and the brightness of the glory of the eternal goodness, who made all for me before you redeemed me.

What praises shall I return to you!

Saturday of the Fifth Week of Lent

A reading on baptism from *The Burial of Christ* by
Myles Coverdale.

See into what poverty Christ submitted himself: he that in his life-time had neither house nor place to lay his head is now covered with strange cloth and laid in a strange sepulcher. By which, though Christ's body was always uncorrupt, we are taught fruitfully to consider the corruption of our body. We are earth, and to the earth we must yield and pay earth again. Ashes we are, and into ashes we must return. Why then do we brag? Why are we proud and high-minded, seeing that shortly we shall become foul dung and carrion? Why do we have such a desire for the wicked world, considering it casts us out so vilely? We should always remember that within a short time we shall be laid down into a foul pit. There is the harbor of all flesh; there lie the rich and poor together in one bed. There is no difference between the noble and base of blood; there neither goods help the rich, nor subtle craft the witty. There the one who a little while ago went bragging up and down in costly apparel, is now an ugly smell to the nose; there the praise and commendation of those who are puffed up in foolish pride departs as the dust before the wind. Thus passes away all mankind, and all flesh falls to the place from whence it came.

Therefore let us learn in this time so to live, and so to subdue the flesh through the Spirit, that when the flesh is corrupted, our soul may be taken into eternal peace and rest. For "all of us who have been baptized into Christ Jesus were baptized into his death. Therefore we have been buried with him by baptism into death, so that, just as Christ was raised from the dead by the glory of the Father, so we too might walk in newness of life."

We must die from the world, and from our own flesh, so that the world may be crucified and dead to us, as we are to the world. The old Adam, who lived and ruled in us, must be subdued and mortified so that only Christ may live and reign in us. We must bury our bodies with myrrh and aloes, that is, with lamentation and sorrow for our sins, with weeping, with fasting, and with abstinence; works of repentance which are bitter to the body. But just as those bitter things, aloes and myrrh, keep the body from corruption, so the cross and adversity sent by God, and borne for God's sake, preserves our flesh from sin.

If we thus die with Christ from the world, and are buried in his death, we shall rise again to a new life, here and in the world to come; and so, as for death, we need not be afraid of it. For the sepulcher is new, and lies in the garden: which symbolizes to us the return to the pleasant garden of paradise, which is opened to us through the death of Christ. For he as a guide has entered in before us so that we also in a new way might escape from death and rise again to a new life. For in the death of Christ death is killed, overcome, and wholly renewed, and altered into a sleep. For we live to God; and our bodies, as the scripture testifies, shall also live again. And this is the reason why the scripture affirms that those who are dead in Christ are asleep.

Until now death mightily and openly reigned, even over those also who had not sinned like Adam, but when the second Adam, namely, Christ, appeared, he purchased life again for mankind, through the death of his flesh, destroying the dominion of death, and rising from death again. Then was death renewed and changed, and became like a sleep: for it does not destroy us for ever, but is a gate and entrance into a better and eternal life. Therefore we have a much more perfect hope of the resurrection in Christ than those of old, who therefore buried the bodies in so costly and honorable a way, because they hoped in the resurrection to come. As for us, we must bestow such cost upon Christ in his members, clothing and feeding the poor, and being ready also to lose all things for his sake.

Being ready to lose all things for Christ.

The Sixth Week of Lent—Holy Week

The Collect for Monday in Holy Week
(Paraphrased)

Almighty God, whose dear, beloved Son
Did not return to you in joy to reign
Nor think the final victory had been won
Until he shared in full our human pain
And therefore did not think to enter in
To heaven's glorious light in victory
Until he triumphed over death and sin
When he was crucified on Calvary,
Be merciful to us, and grant that we
Who follow now the way that Jesus trod
And take his cross and bear it faithfully
May find it brings us life and peace, Lord God,
Whom with the Son and Spirit we adore,
This day and always, now and evermore.

–Christopher L. Webber

The Sunday of the Passion–Palm Sunday

A reading from a sermon by Richard Meux Benson on the theme of redemption.

If worldly goals have engrossed our energies, if we have made any of them a real end and aim in life, we have given ourselves up to slavery, we have fallen into bondage to that which by God's original appointment could not rightfully be our Lord, we have lived for a dead world, not for a living God. But we have been ransomed from these things. Let us therefore be quit, for ever quit, of every earthly aim. Christ is our one Lord, our eternal Lord, the Lord in whose service our happiness consists. Christ is the Lord "whose service is perfect freedom," for in his service all our energies are free to be exercised for all the true purposes ordained by God as conducive to our eternal welfare. Truly we are a ransomed people!

Regarding all things from this standing point, we can know ourselves as the Lord's free people; "For freedom Christ has set us free." The changing world flits past us—unsubstantial, however fascinating—a dream, though it seems like a necessity. We live in freedom from it, if we live to God. We must be altogether detached from it, if we would be one with Christ. Yes, we are here only strangers and pilgrims, and "our citizenship is in heaven, and it is from there that we are expecting a Savior, the Lord Jesus Christ."

Oh! what a world shall that be where the children of God meet in the full manifestation of their freedom, around the throne of their Almighty Father and King! How differently should we estimate all earthly affection, if we looked forward to that time! We must be dead to all social relationships, and know the dearest ties of natural affection only in the glorifying, sanctifying power of Christ's resurrection if we would realize that glory. The closest bonds of earth will crumble into dust. One bond alone can knit us permanently together, the bond of union in Christ. As members of the old human family under the dominion of death, we could not hold each other's love longer than that stern tyrant gave us leave. Affections sanctified in Christ are strong forever. Christ has redeemed us from death. The outer differences of earth will crumble away as a worthless husk. Those whom we may have known and loved will rise in glory only by reason of having lived in Christ. In Christ then let us learn to love one another. Oh, learn a love superior to all mere social ties or artificial distinctions! Wealth, talent, beauty, influence, are apt to enslave us while they win our affections. Think of the time when they will be past and gone. Think of the time when poverty and abjectness will no longer compass the members of the Crucified. Love one another now, as you will love another, if you are mutually capable of love, hereafter. Love one another for the reason which will then awaken love, then share in one common redemption. Love one another in the strength by which love will operate between you, the renewing energy of the love of Christ. Love one another after the pattern of love whose glory will then be revealed, the true, self-sacrificing love of a Savior's Cross. Love one another now in such a way as you may hope to survive the certain catastrophe of death. Love one another with a love that is pure and free, the love of the redeemed, the love of the heavenly, as conscious that you are already called to act one towards another in the fellowship of a Savior's life, which abides for ever. So resolve indeed to "regard no one from a human point of view." A Savior's death is between you and all earthly things. A Savior's death enshrines around you all that should be loved. Christ in heaven is the source of your strength. The divine life of Christ is your exceeding great reward. The heart of Christ is that in which you may—in which alone you must—learn the true law of a love that shall be free and operative in the immortality of God.

Christ is the source of your strength.

Monday of Holy Week

A reading from a meditation on God's love by Elizabeth Rowe.

Break, break, insensitive heart; let confusion cover me and darkness, black as my own guilt, surround me. Lord, what a monster have I become. How hateful to myself for offending you; how much more detestable to you against whom I have offended! Why have I provoked the God on whom my being every moment depends, the God who, out of nothing, advanced me to a reasonable and immortal nature, and put me in a position to be happy for ever; the God whose goodness has run parallel with my life; who has preserved me in a thousand dangers, and kept me from the ruin I courted, even while I repined at the providence that saved me.

Could I consider you as my enemy, I might forgive myself, but when I consider you as my best friend, my tender father, the sustainer of my life and author of my happiness, good God! what a monstrous thing do I appear who have sinned against you! Could I charge you with severity, or call your laws rigorous and unjust, I would have some excuse, but I am silenced there by the conviction of my own reason, which assents to all your precepts as just and holy. But to heighten my guilt, I have violated the sacred rules I approve, I have provoked the justice I fear, and offended the purity I adore. Yet still there are higher aggravations of my iniquity; and what gives me the utmost confusion is that I have sinned against unbounded love and goodness. Horrid ingratitude; here lies the emphasis of my folly and misery; the sense of this torments me, can I not say, as much as the dread of hell, or the fears of losing heaven? Your love and tender compassion, the late pleasing subjects of my thoughts, have on this account become my terror.

The titles of an enemy and a judge scarcely sound more painful to my ears than those of a friend and a benefactor which so shamefully enhance my guilt: those sacred names confound and terrify my soul because they furnish my conscience with the most exquisite reproaches. The thoughts of such goodness abused, and such clemency affronted, seem to me almost as insupportable as those of thy wrath and severity. Oh! whither shall I turn? I dare not look upward, the sun and stars upbraid me there; if I look downwards, the fields and fountains take their Creator's part and heaven and earth conspire to aggravate my sins. Those common blessings tell me how much I am indebted to thy bounty; but, Lord, when I recall thy particular favors I am utterly confounded. What numerous instances could I recount? Nor has my rebellion yet shut up the fountain of thy grace, for yet I breathe, and yet I live, and live to implore a pardon: heaven is still open, and the throne of God accessible. But oh! with what confidence can I approach it? what motives can I urge, but such as carry my own condemnation in them?

Shall I urge your former pity and indulgence? This were to plead against myself; and yet your clemency, that clemency which I have abused, is the best argument I can bring: your grace and clemency, as revealed in Jesus, the son of thy love, the blessed reconciler of God and man.

Oh whither has my folly reduced me? with what words shall I choose to address you? "Pardon my iniquity, O Lord, for it is great." Surprising argument! yet this will magnify your goodness, and yield me an eternal theme to praise you: it will add an emphasis to all my grateful songs, and tune my harp to everlasting harmony. The ransomed of the Lord shall join with me, while this glorious instance of your grace excites their wonder, and my unbounded gratitude; thus shall your glory be exalted.

I have provoked the justice I fear.

Tuesday of Holy Week

A reading from a sermon by John Keble on the theme of "Christ's Own Preparation for His Passion."

As he did on the Sunday of this week so he did on all the following days, until the Friday: the morning and daylight hours he spent in the temple, teaching, instructing the multitude and his disciples, and warning his malicious enemies, who were all the while watching him; and the nights he spent on the Mount of Olives: in what sort of employment, we may guess, both from what we read of him before, and from what followed near the end of the week. We read of him in the early part of the Gospel, when he first began to preach, that after a very hard day's work of healing human bodies and instructing their souls, rising up "a great while before day," he departed and went "into a solitary place," and was there praying when his disciples came to look for him. Again, after the miracle of the loaves, "He departed again into a mountain himself alone," and was there until the fourth watch of the night, that is, three in the morning. Another time, after much disputing with his enemies, and long teaching in the temple, the Pharisees went "every man to his own house": they had houses to go to, with plenty of ease and all sorts of comforts awaiting them. But Jesus went to the Mount of Olives. He chose not to have any home where he might lay his head. After his days had been days of charity, he would have his nights nights of devotion.

As it was during his ministry, so it was, still more, when that ministry was drawing to an end. The very day before his Passion, having first eaten the Passover with his disciples, and given them those instructions which we read in St. John, he went out into a garden, the Garden of Gethsemane, on the slope of the Mount of Olives, where he had often come with his disciples; and there he was praying, when the soldiers and Judas came upon him.

Our Lord's preparation then for his sufferings lay in these two things: active practical duties by day, and earnest devotion and meditation by night. Now that, by which he prepared himself for the Cross itself, and the grave, and all his mysterious sufferings, the same must be the best preparation for his people also, when they are celebrating the memory and likeness of those sufferings. For what is the purpose of the Holy Church Universal in appointing this particular time of year, during which for so many days we are to follow him step by step, through all the stages of his bitter passion first, and then of his triumphant victory over death? Of course, what is meant is, that we, by the help of God's Holy Spirit, should make what happened to him as present to us, and as near to us, as ever we can; that we should, as St. Paul says, "have the mind of Christ"; that, when Good Friday comes, we should spend that solemn day with some faint touch at least of his heavenly patience, charity, and self-denial; that the Cross should not be lifted up for us in vain, but that we should go out of ourselves, forget and renounce ourselves, and turn all our faith and hope and love towards our Divine and only Savior, as Mary Magdalene did, and the other holy women, when they stood by beholding his death. This, I say, is part at least of the Church's purpose in having such a day as Good Friday, and such a week as Passion Week, to humble and chasten our minds, by way of preparation for that awe-filled day.

There must be a preparation of heart and mind or the word spoken in our ears, the wonders wrought in our sight, will fail to come home to us. And if this be the case in respect of all Divine institutions, much more of so great a thing as the sacrifice of God's Son, which is the salvation of the whole world.

There must be a preparation of heart and mind.

Wednesday of Holy Week

A reading from a sermon by Rowan Williams, archbishop of Canterbury, on the Parable of the Unforgiving Servant (Matthew 18:23–35).

People will often talk about forgiveness in a way that suggests that forgiveness is the same as acquittal—as if it simply obliterated the past, as if it were an arbitrary fiat which unties all the knots we are bound in by simply pretending certain things haven't happened. But if we have been badly hurt by someone, then whatever happens the scars and memories will still be there, even if we "forgive" them. And if we have hurt someone, the same is true: we may be "forgiven," but we can see the effects of what we have done, perhaps for years after. If forgiveness is forgetting, then it is a mockery of the depth and seriousness of the suffering that human beings inflict on each other.

No, we need something more positive to say about forgiveness. The occasions when we feel genuinely forgiven are the moments when we feel, not that someone doesn't care what we do, but that someone *does* care what we do because he or she loves us and that love is strong enough to cope with and survive the hurt we have done. Forgiveness of that sort is creative because it reveals new dimensions to a relationship, new depths, new possibilities. It recognizes the reality of the past, the irreversibility of things, the seriousness of damage done, but then it is all the more joyful and hopeful because of that. This kind of love doesn't have illusions. It can look at and fully *feel* my weaknesses, and still say, "I love you."

But are there wounds never to be healed, personally as well as globally? After all, our love is *not* very strong. It is hardly surprising if we come to a point where we say, "I can't take that. That is the end of love." Is forgiveness to depend on this, on our hopeless, inept struggles to love?

The reply of the gospel is "no." Forgiveness is not only a matter to be settled among ourselves—or left unsettled because of our inadequacies. It is God's affair too. And the good news of Christianity is that, since God suffers human pain, since God is the victim of human injury, then there is beyond all our sin a love that is inexhaustible. So God can always survive the hurt we do to God, whenever we turn to him in sorrow and longing, after we have done some injury, this love is still there, waiting for us, a home whose door is always open. *Whatever* we do can never shut that door to God's merciful acceptance. The only thing that can keep us out is the refusal to ask for and trust in that mercy.

And the gospel proclaims all this in virtue of the cross of Jesus. Without that, we cannot begin to understand the forgiveness of sins. Jesus crucified is God crucified; so we believe. Jesus is the total and final embodiment in history of God's loving mercy; and so this cross is a unique, terrible, extreme act of violence—a summary of all sin. It represents the human rejection of love. And not even *that* can destroy God; with the wounds of the cross still disfiguring his body, he returns out of hell to his disciples and wishes them peace. There is our hope—the infinite *resource* of God's love, the relationship with God's creatures that no sin can finally unmake. God cares what we do because God suffers what we do. God is forever wounded, but forever loving. The possibilities of our relationship with God are indeed "new every morning."

So our sins become not stopping points, but starting points. They can be the occasions of constantly fresh, constantly wider visions of the grace of God. It's often been said, boldly, that the saints in heaven rejoice over their sins, because through them they have been brought to greater and greater understanding of the endless endurance of God's love, to the knowledge that beyond every failure God's creative mercy still waits. We have a future because of this grace.

We have a future because of God's grace.

Maundy Thursday

A reading from a sermon preached before King James I on Ash Wednesday, 1619, by Lancelot Andrewes on the text: "Yet even now, says the LORD, return to me with all your heart, with fasting, with weeping, and with mourning; rend your hearts and not your clothing. Return to the LORD, your God" (Joel 2:12–13).

This Lenten turning involves not only the brain; no, heart and all must turn: not only the face for shame, nor the feet for fear, but the heart for true hatred of sin also. With the heart, and the whole heart, and not so as to divide the heart from the body nor to divide the heart in itself. The devil, to hinder us from true turning, turns himself into various shapes, suggesting, "Do not turn at all; you are doing well enough. Then, if you must turn, turn wherever you will but not to God. If to God, leave your heart behind you and turn. If with the heart, with some few broken affections, but not entirely."

When the heart is thus parceled out, it is easy to see how one would play with fire and not be burned, touch pitch and not be defiled, love peril and not perish in it, dallying with our conversion: turning like a door on its hinges to open and shut, and shut and open again. Be bold to say to such a one that such is not the way of conversion.

It is easy to see when one goes about turning with the whole heart: set down what must be done and they will do it: not come near the place where sin dwells, restrain the wandering of the sense by which sin is awakened, but chiefly corrupt company where sin resorts. For conversion has no greater enemy than conversing with those of whom our heart tells us there is neither faith nor fear of God in them.

And so may we turn, and such may all our conversion be: voluntary, without compulsion; to God without declining; with the whole heart, without purpose of return.

And so now at the last again: "rend your hearts." First and last, to the heart we come. For indeed a meal may be missed, a tear or two may fall, and the heart not be affected for all that. As in conversion, the purpose of amendment must proceed from the heart. So in our contrition, the sorrow and anger for our turning away must pierce to the heart; the heart must suffer.

And do it now. As in a circle, I return to the first word "now" which gives us our time. When all is done, we must bring this to a time present. Now is the only sure part of our time. That which is past is come and gone. That which is to come may possibly never come. Of tomorrow, this evening, an hour hence, we have no assurance. "Now," therefore; or if not "now," as near "now" with as little distance from it as may be; if not this day, then this time now coming.

For even though no time is bad to turn in, yet since many times do pass over our heads and still we cannot find a time to do it in, the Church, as I said, to reduce the diffuseness of our repentance in general to the certainty of some one set time, has placed this "now" on the time now begun and commends it to us for our turning to God.

Perform it then, and when our turn is done, our repentance will bring about God's. If we turn from the evil we have done, God will turn from us the evil that should have been done to us. We shall turn God's very style, and so make a change in God.

We shall be no losers by it. A less sorrow shall turn away a greater by a great deal. Weigh the endless sorrow we shall escape but it admits no comparison. The contrition is for an hour; the consolation is for ever and ever.

To this there belongs a blessing: Blessed are those who thus mourn. It is so set by the Church that our Lent shall end with Easter, the highest and most solemn feast of the year: the memory of Christ's rising and the pledge of our blessed and joyful resurrection.

Rend your heart.

Good Friday

A reading from a sermon on the crucifixion by Mark Frank.

All tongues are too little to speak of "Jesus Christ, and him crucified"; all knowledge not sufficient to make us know him, and teach him as we should. We need all tongues and knowledge—all words and eloquence, to set it forth.

Well then, at least let us see what it is "to know . . . Jesus Christ, and him crucified." St. Paul makes it his only glory; with a "May I never boast of anything except the cross of our Lord Jesus Christ." Indeed, all our happiness flows from this: the wound in his side is the hole of the rock in which alone the soul can lie secure; the water that issued out from it is the only fluid to cleanse it in; the blood is the only drink it lives by; the wood of the cross, is the only tree of life; the title of it is better to us than all the titles of the earth; the reproach of it, better than all the honors of the world; the pains of it, sweeter than all the pleasures under heaven; the wounds, better cordials and restoratives to a sick soul than all the physic nature or skill affords.

There is not a grain of that holy wood that is not of more worth than all the grains of gold that the Indies can afford. There is not a vein in that crucified body of Jesus that does not run full with heavenly comfort to us. There is nothing in "Christ crucified," but humanity glorified. Who, indeed, would not be determined to fix all knowledge here—to dwell here for ever?

This you all know as well as I. Yet I must tell you, you do not know it as you should, if you do not sit down sometimes and determine your thoughts upon it; unless you sadly meditate, and thankfully think upon it; unless you value the meditations and discourses of it above all other thoughts, all other talk; unless you set aside other business ever and anon to contemplate this.

But, "to know Christ Jesus crucified," is more than this; it is in St. Paul's meaning, "to be crucified with him," to "take up our cross and follow him"; to make profession of him, though we are sure to come to execution by it; to go with him as St. Thomas exhorts, even if we die with him, to be willing to suffer anything for him; to deny our own wisdom and reputation, and ourselves, for his service; to be content to be counted fools for his sake; our very wisdom and preaching, foolishness; if we may save any by it, to count all as nothing, so we may know him, and be known of him.

This we speak, this we preach, this we profess, this we determine upon with St. Paul to know, to think, to speak, to teach, to preach, to profess this, and nothing else, ever crying out to him "This crucified Jesus is my God and all, this Christ crucified is my God and all"; all my thoughts, all my heart, all my knowledge, all my profession; he is all in all, I know nothing else, I value nothing else; I know him though never so disfigured by his wounds; I will acknowledge him, though in the midst of the thieves; I am not ashamed of him, though full of spittle and reproach; I will profess him, though all run from him. Alas! I know not anything worth knowing, if they take him away.

And yet to know him has one degree more. So to know Christ, then, is to become like him; to know him as a Savior is to be a savior to the poor and needy, to deliver the widow and fatherless from the hand of the oppressor; to know him to be crucified is to crucify our affections and lusts. Thus we know him as he is here, and by so knowing him here, we shall at last come to know him hereafter; where we shall know him perfectly, know him glorified for here knowing him crucified, and all things then with him; for now not knowing anything but him, know God, and happiness, and eternal glory, and ourselves partakers in them all.

This crucified Jesus is my God and my all.

Holy Saturday

A reading on the descent into hell from *I Believe: Sermons on the Apostles' Creed* by G. A. Studdert-Kennedy.

In the descent into hell Christ's trumpet calls us to the parting of the ways. Here for the first time the Creed swings out into another world; death is not the end, it says, there is more to come. Life is more than a matter of life and death. Good and evil, truth and falsehood are not mere matters of welfare and happiness in this world, their effects and consequences reach out into another sphere. The Creed calls us to bet our lives on the fact that five minutes after death we shall be conscious, thinking, feeling, knowing, sorrowing, and joying. It calls us to believe that there is another sphere of life which lies so close to this that within three minutes from now I could be there if I would. It only needs a revolver or some prussic acid, and I could if I would, be standing in that other land.

But there is still more behind this clause. There surrounds it a Christian tradition that the Spirit of Jesus, when it passed into paradise, was not idle there and did not sleep, but spread abroad in paradise, as he spread abroad on earth, the great good news of God's eternal love and of salvation yet to come. Whether Our Lord told St. Peter this after he was risen from the tomb, or whether Christians who knew Christ felt that this was a necessity that followed from the love of God as they had found it revealed in him, because otherwise all the countless millions who had lived and died before he walked on the earth and lived his life and died his death to bring new life into the world would have been ignorant and in the dark and would have remained without hope of salvation, eternally lost—whether, I say, the tradition sprang from Christ himself or sprang from the meditations of Christians on the love of God recorded in Christ, it stands there as part of the great gospel, and it does seem to be legitimate for us to draw conclusions from it. I conclude that Christ passed into paradise to meet not only the penitent thief but the unrepentant thief as well. He went to preach to those "who in former times did not obey" because, for reasons beyond their power to control, they had never seen Christ. The reason in their case was that they were not born in time, but there are a million other reasons that operate in the world to prevent others from ever seeing Christ, reasons which are beyond their power to control. Thousands of others have lived since Jesus died and never known his name. The line sweeps out to the ends of the world, East and West, North and South, and gathers the staggering multitude in, and the message of the cross comes for them: neither length nor breadth nor height nor depth nor death itself can separate them from the life of Christ which passes knowledge. Even beyond the grave there is hope. The God of Life goes on striving in the after world; death is a crisis but not an ending.

There are those who simply cannot respond, and for them the message comes that he passed into paradise and that just as the crucifixion is an act in time revealing a process in eternity, so is the descent into hell. Just as it is true not merely that he suffered once, but that he suffers still to serve the human race, so it is true not merely that he descended into hell, but that he for ever descends into the depths to seek and to save that which is lost.

Once more this clause rings out the challenge to the belief in the everlasting love and calls us out on the journey, upwards and onwards through life and through death to the Jesus of goodness, following the star of Bethlehem that sets in Calvary's hill only to rise and shine again more brightly as the lodestar of the human race.

There is no positive proof, there is nothing that can compel certainty, about the existence of that other world. It remains a venture of faith. And so once more the gallant Creed calls us to stake our lives on the assumption that God will not leave us in the grave nor suffer God's children to see corruption, but that we shall pass on to paradise.

Death is a crisis but not an ending.

Easter Week

Fear Not

"Fear not because of me," the angel said;
"The stone has been rolled back and he who died,
The Lord you seek, is risen from the dead

And those they sent to guard the tomb have fled
In panic from the one they crucified.
Fear not because of me," the angel said,

"Nor let your hearts be filled again with dread
Of sin and death for they have been denied;
The Lord you seek is risen from the dead

And he will go to Galilee ahead
Of you, and now he will be glorified.
Fear not because of me," the angel said,

"Nor fear the powers of this world; instead,
Go tell the world and publish far and wide:
The Lord you seek is risen from the dead

And now you will be comforted and fed
And he will go with you and be your guide.
Fear not because of me," the angel said,
"The Lord you seek is risen from the dead."

                              –Christopher L. Webber

Easter Day

A reading from "The Resurrection of Christ" by
Myles Coverdale.

The evangelists most diligently set forth to us the resurrection of Christ, as a thing necessary, profitable, and joyful to all faithful believers. For in the resurrection we see how Christ is exalted, and what hope we have in him. But this resurrection the evangelists teach as human understanding may comprehend it. For if Christ had suddenly at once opened himself to his disciples, they would have taken it for a plain fantasy and vision, as they did when the Lord appeared to them upon the water. Therefore the evangelists describe the matter very distinctly and in sundry ways, so that no one can be able to suspect any deceit. First, how the women and men came to the sepulcher, looked, and went in; and how they viewed everything thoroughly, not once, but often and many times; the clothes wherein the Lord was wrapped, the headkerchief, everything folded together in its separate place; and how they saw and perceived that the body was not there, that the sepulcher was open, the stone rolled away, and how the angels and heavenly spirits testified that he was risen again. Yet for all this they are weak, and believe it not steadfastly; but are as yet in a doubt. Thus God permits them to waver, and to be feeble of belief, and does not thoroughly persuade them immediately, and that is done for our sakes.

The wisdom of God leads them still by little and little, to make them stronger, declaring to them certain assured evidences; as that the body was not in the sepulcher, but that the clothes lay there wrapped together; for these were undoubted tokens that he was risen up again. For if any-one had taken him out of the sepulcher, as Magdalene thought, he could not have had so much time and leisure as to loose up the bands and to undo the clothes from the body; but would have taken and carried away the clothes and body together: for the clothes stuck fast to the body, partly by reason of the blood, and partly through the aloes and myrrh that the body was dressed withal. But for all this they are still weak and in doubt until such time as the Lord himself strengthens them. Thus God is revealed to whom, and when, God wills. For though we see sometimes many great and wonderful works, though we read and hear much of the scriptures, yet our heart remains still ignorant, nor does the doctrine take effect, till Christ open it, and till he himself is the schoolmaster.

Thus we learn also to know and honor Christ now no more after the flesh, and to show no corporal outward service to his person. In spirit will he be worshiped, with the faith and love of the inward mind. If anything bodily is done by us, it should be done to the poor, and to the neighbor that has need of it. Thus may faith and love well use some outward things, not to do service to God, but to ourselves or to our neighbor. When we take and minister bread and wine in the supper, distributing and eating it, this is not done principally to declare a service to God, but somewhat to stimulate our outward senses and flesh by exterior signs so that we may better consider and ponder the grace of God declared to us in the death of Jesus Christ, and that we may lift up our minds to Christ, the heavenly food and living bread, who inwardly feeds us with his flesh, and nourishes us with his blood.

Oh, how great a grace is this! Oh, how high is the glory that here is promised us in Christ! The only-begotten Son of God descended and became human for us, that we, so much as is possible for our nature, should ascend up to his Godhead. He descended down low so that when we are humbled, he might receive and exalt us to his own promotion. He that of nature is the Lord, took upon him the shape of a servant, that of us who naturally were bond-servants, he might make us God's children. Forasmuch then as he became human, to make us God's children of godly grace, he took upon him that which is ours to give us that which is his. Therefore he calls us brothers and sisters and makes his own Father common to us; so that he is also our Father and our God:

How great a grace is this!

Monday in Easter Week

A reading from a sermon by Morgan Dix entitled "The Morning of Eternity," on the text: "Just after daybreak, Jesus stood on the beach; but the disciples did not know that it was Jesus" (John 21:4).

No season of the Christian year speaks to the soul as does the Easter Tide. It is the beautiful season of the year, when the winter is ended and all things bud forth; the graves and sleeping-places of the dust are broken up and the beauty of the floral kingdom comes back to us in the fresh glory of living green and painted leaves and with the perfume of the incense-breathing gardens of spring. Now best may the gospel of immortality be preached, when ten thousand times ten thousand witnesses confirm the word; when bud and leaf and flower, when every little branch that swells with new life of the spring, and every brook that frees itself of ice and resumes the song of the past, and every gentle bird and beast, and tiny creatures of the dust, and all that have life and health, seem to rejoice in the morning of their returning day; now comes to us the gospel of immortality, attested by a great cloud of witnesses in earth, sea, and sky, and vouched for by the deeper tones of years that are past; by the testimony of all ages since Christ was here; by the voice of those who have lived and died believing that, to God, there are no dead, that "for to him all are alive." This is the thing which has been most surely believed among us; the event from which all else is reckoned backwards and forwards; the stay of those on their journey, the inspiration of genius, the melody of music, the strength of manners and morals, the support and consolation of the mourning heart. From the natural and the moral world, the world of history and art, the worlds of mind, of matter, and of religion, come voices announcing that Christ is risen from the dead and become the first fruits of them that sleep.

Since this is so, and all seems truly tuned in the key of spiritual joy and gladness, one might expect to find in the Holy Gospels pictures of rare and singular beauty where the resurrection of the Lord is in hand. It is especially so in the Gospel of Saint John. The symbol of that evangelist is the eagle; type of the lofty spiritual character of his work, the far flight upward, above the every-day and commonplace plane, the keen unblenched look into the face of the mysterious realm. And hence in the last two chapters of his gospel, where the apostle treats of the life and acts of the Risen Lord, we find, as might have been expected, that all seems weird and beautiful, with the beauty of another world and another life. The gospel seems to end; it has not ended; one more chapter comes; it scarcely belongs to what went before; the record is hardly of this world; all is strange, and mystical, as if relating to a day that began but never closed. As we read there comes over us the impression of an invisible presence before which individuals move as in a dream; one is near them, but where, they know not. Imagine what it is to be in such a state. Suppose that some unearthly being were here in whom your destiny was completed and in whom your very life was wrapped up; one whom you could not see yet knew to be at hand; who might at any instant appear; some spirit or more than spirit, felt though invisible, ever and anon disclosing himself, and then vanishing: how strange the life that should be passed in such society with supernatural manifestations ever imminent, and in hourly expectation of some new turn of events. Thus did the apostles in Galilee pass those Forty Days called in the Church by the name of Great; the days which came between the Rising of the Lord and his Ascending. In the spring-tide and in a region full of beauty, God taught them, and us through them, that human beings shall surely live for evermore with Christ, and that death has no dominion over the children of God.

Death has no dominion over the children of God.

Tuesday in Easter Week

A reading from a sermon by Morgan Dix entitled "The Morning of Eternity," on the text: "Just after daybreak, Jesus stood on the beach; but the disciples did not know that it was Jesus" (John 21:4).

In the marvelous story of the morning by the lake, there is a prophecy in symbol; it is that of the revelation of the last days; what mankind has been desiring and hoping for, as far back as human records run, is here shown forth as at last fulfilled. "For I know that my Redeemer lives, and that at the last he will stand upon the earth." That strong cry out of the far, far past, is answered by the vision on the lake. When the night was gone, and "Just after daybreak, Jesus stood on the beach"; Christ is no longer with them in the ship, nor ever shall be thenceforth; he stands on the shore; they lift up their eyes and behold; they must go there to him. The voyage of life is done; its storms are laid forever; the work is finished. There is no night any longer, nor time, nor days and years; "everything old has passed away; see, everything has become new!" It is an indescribable vision of what is to be hereafter; a prophecy in action; the turmoil, the care, the labors of time and this mortal life yield to the influences of the new day of God; the everlasting springtide comes; the Easter of Eternity is kept; and the tired and weary go home to Christ, and find on the shore of the happy land, the fullness of rest and peace.

Strange to say, there is comfort in this thought, that they did not know the Lord at that moment. When you are distressed because you cannot see clearly, remember to your comfort, that they, his own apostles, his own most intimate friends, who loved him with supreme devotion, who talked more of him than of aught else, who longed to see him and be with him where he was, did not know him when he stood before them on the shore. It may be so with you. The cares of this world, the duties and labors of your life, errors which cloud the human intellect and infirmities which weaken the physical system; these and other similar causes may have obscured your vision, and depressed your spirit: but they will pass away, and at the last you will see the Lord, and know even as you are known.

Since that morning by the sea, what then took place has been repeated and realized in myriads of instances, among those who have followed and loved our Lord Jesus Christ. It is repeated and realized in the death of his saints. Let us pray that it be thus with ourselves and those whom we love in the world. Truly our life is but a brief voyage, and generally a fretful one; we have much to do and little time; there is hard work for all, and much of that work seems to disappoint. The fields yield no meat; we toil all night and take nothing, the unstable and the fearful are apt to lose faith and heart. Let it not be so with us: a little while, and we shall see; a little patience, a little longer battle with groundless fears, and the victory over self will be complete. Fight the good fight of faith; persevere to the end; do not despair; hold fast to him whom the clouds and darkness still hide; and when your hour comes, all shall be well; the Figure which they saw so long ago, your eyes shall also behold with joy, the Figure of the Savior whom you have believed and to whom you made your prayer in your own darkness; he shall be there, his glorious loving face turned toward you, his arms open; and then you shall know for yourself that your Redeemer lives, and that it is he who stands before you on the eternal shore.

At the last you will see the Lord.

Wednesday in Easter Week

A reading on the resurrection from *The Wicket Gate* by G. A. Studdert-Kennedy.

The last certainty is the certainty of death. It is the one thing of which we can be sure. We may try to forget it, but it will not forget us. Nor can we ever really forget it until we have faced it and come to a decision about it. In the midst of life we are in death, unless we know that in the midst of death we are in life.

The more we grow in the love of Beauty, Truth, and Goodness, the more completely human we become, the more intense must grow our hunger for immortality and our abhorrence of death. The idea that belief in immortality is an ancient doctrine fast losing ground is an exact reversing of the facts, it is a completely modern doctrine which the growth of human personality and its firmer hold on a wider world makes inevitable. It is the human infancy that cries, "How good is human life, the mere living, how fit to employ all the heart and the soul and the senses for ever in joy." It is the fully developed human being who cries, "Whom have I in heaven but you? And there is nothing on earth that I desire other than you."

Faith in eternal life is and must be the logical conclusion—using logic in its fullest human sense—of the instinct of self-preservation. As we grow, so grows that divine discontent that severs us completely from the rest of the animal creation and bids us reach out to fuller and fuller life. We can find endless reasons to justify the instinctive craving, but it is the instinct that sets us reasoning, and unless the world is a fraud, that instinct points to something real by which it can be satisfied.

The shadowy hosts whom Virgil pictured in the underworld, crowding by the river bank and stretching out their hands in longing for the farther shore, held out their hands backward to the life that they had left, not forward to the life which was to come. But as humanity grows, the hands turn around and are stretched out to the future, not back to the past. We become conscious that the most perfect things in life like Love, Beauty, and Truth fall short of perfection. And yet God has given us so much, can we believe that God will not give more?

From the purely intellectual point of view there are many sound philosophical arguments for eternal life. But certainty only comes with certainty about God and God's love. We can never reach the point of victory and triumph over death until we reach the heart of the Father in Jesus Christ, and it is that triumphant certainty that we need not for the future only but for the present. We cannot live in this life aright unless we see it in its true perspective, see it as the foreground of eternity. Apart from that we tend to see all things in a wrong proportion; big things become little and little things become big and we labor for that which is not bread. There is no peace for us as long as we live in the Valley of the Shadow of Death. It is only the tender mercy of our God whereby the Day-spring from on high can visit us to give light to those who sit in darkness and the shadow of death, only through God's mercy that our human feet can be guided into the paths of peace. Apart from this triumphant certainty life becomes vulgar and sordid. When the shadow of death falls over all the beauty of the world, the hunger for life in us is so strong that it tends to brutalize and drive us to grasp at everything we can get without caring how we get it, and life tends to become a struggle of swine about the trough— a struggle in which there is no tenderness and no mercy.

Unless then life mocks us and has no meaning, the instinct for self-preservation must have its perfect work and must lead to truth, not falsehood. The Christian hypothesis is that life is as good as God revealed in Christ and that behind the Cross there is ever and always the resurrection. And it is only by taking that hypothesis and living life as though it were true, flinging ourselves upon it recklessly in the faith that God keeps the good wine until the last, that we can come to that triumphant certainty which destroys death and makes us sure that in the midst of death we are in life everlasting.

In the midst of death we are in life.

Thursday in Easter Week

A sermon by John Newton on the text, "But in fact Christ has been raised from the dead, the first fruits of those who have died" (1 Corinthians 15:20).

The disciples were neither ashamed, nor afraid, to proclaim his gospel, and to invite and enjoin sinners everywhere to put their trust in him. Otherwise, they had nothing to expect; but such treatment as they actually met with, for professing their belief of his resurrection; and especially for the pains they took to publish it: first among the people who had put him to death, and afterwards among the Heathens. It required no great sagacity to foresee that this doctrine would be an offence to the Jews, and foolishness to the Greeks. They were, in fact, despised, hated, opposed, and persecuted, wherever they went; and those who espoused their cause, were immediately exposed to a participation in their sufferings. Nor was there the least probability that this event could be otherwise. There have been many imposters, but we cannot conceive that any set of men, would deliberately, and by consent, contrive an imposture, which in the nature, of the thing, could procure nothing to them, or to their followers, but contempt, stripes, imprisonment, and death.

Even if we could for a moment suppose them capable of so wild and wicked an undertaking, as, under pretense of the service of God, to provoke and dare the hatred of mankind, by asserting and propagating an offensive falsehood, it would be impossible, upon those grounds, to account for the success which they met with. If this counsel and cause had not been of God, it must have come to nought.

But by preaching Jesus and his resurrection, in defiance of all the art and rage of their enemies, they mightily prevailed over the established customs and age-old prejudices of mankind, and brought multitudes into the belief of their doctrine, against all disadvantages. The Lord confirmed their word with signs following. The miracles which were wrought in the name of Jesus, were numerous, notable, and undeniable. And the moral effects of their preaching, though too frequent and universal to be styled miraculous, were such as can only be ascribed with reason to a divine power. The pillars of Paganism, the superstitions of idol worship, though, in every country, connected and incorporated with the frame of civil government, and guarded for ages, not more by popular veneration, than for reasons of state, were very soon shaken, and, in no great space of time, subverted. Within about two hundred years after Tacitus had described the Christians as the objects of universal contempt and hatred, Christianity became the established religion of the empire. And in a letter of Pliny to Trajan on the subject, we have indisputable evidence that even in the time of Tacitus, hated, vilified, and persecuted, as the Christians were, their religion so greatly prevailed, that in many places the idol temples were almost deserted.

But the proof of the resurrection of Christ, which is the most important and satisfactory of any, does not depend upon arguments and historical evidence, with which multitudes of true Christians are unacquainted, but is, in its own nature, equally convincing in all ages, and equally open to all capacities. Those who have found the gospel to be the power of God to the salvation of their souls, have the witness in themselves and are very sure, that the doctrine, which enlightened their understandings, awakened their consciences, delivered them from the guilt and dominion of sin, brought them into a state of peace and communion with God, and inspired them with a bright and glorious hope of eternal life, must be true. They know that the Lord is risen indeed, because they are made partakers of the power of his resurrection, and have experienced a change in themselves, which could only be wrought by the influence of that Holy Spirit which Jesus is exalted to bestow. And many believers, though not qualified to dispute with philosophers and sceptics, upon their own learned ground, can put them to shame and to silence, by the integrity and purity of their conduct, by their patience and cheerfulness under afflictions, and would especially silence them, if they were eye-witnesses of the composure and elevation of spirit, with which true believers in a risen Savior welcome the approach of death.

They know that the Lord is risen because of a change in themselves.

Friday in Easter Week

A reading from *Footsteps of the Master* by Harriet Beecher Stowe.

There is something wonderfully poetic in the simple history given by the different evangelists of the resurrection of our Lord. It is like a calm, serene morning after a night of thunder and tempest. Those devoted women, in whose hearts love out-lived both faith and hope, rose while it was yet dark and set out with their spices and perfumes to go and pay their best tribute of affection and reverence to the dead.

They were under fear of persecution and death; they knew the grave was sealed and watched by those who had slain their Lord, but they were determined to go. There was the inconsiderate hardihood of love in their undertaking, and the artless helplessness of their inquiry, "Who will roll away the stone from the door?" shows the desperation of their enterprise. Yet they could not but believe that by prayers or tears or official payment—in some way—that stone should be rolled away.

Arrived on the spot, they saw that the sepulcher was open and empty, and Mary Magdalene, with the impulsive haste and earnestness which marks her character, ran back to the house of John, where were the mother of Jesus, and Peter, and astonished them with the tidings, "They have taken the Lord out of the tomb, and we do not know where they have laid him."

Nothing is said of the Mother in this scene. Probably she was utterly worn out and exhausted by the dreadful scenes of the day before and incapable of further exertion. But Peter and John started immediately for the sepulcher. Meanwhile the two other women went into the sepulcher and stood here perplexed till suddenly they saw a vision of celestial forms, radiant in immortal youth and clothed in white. One said,

"Do not be afraid; I know that you are looking for Jesus who was crucified. He is not here; for he has been raised, as he said. Come, see the place where he lay."

And they remembered his words.

Furthermore, the friendly spirit bids them go and tell the disciples and Peter that their Master is risen from the dead and is going before them into Galilee—there they shall see him. And charged with this message, the women had fled from the tomb just as Peter and John came up.

The delicacies of character are strikingly shown in the brief record. John outruns Peter, stoops down and looks into the sepulcher, but that species of reticence which always appears in him controls him here— he hesitates to enter the sacred place. Now, however, comes Peter, impetuous, ardent, determined, and passes right into the tomb.

There is a touch of homelike minuteness in the description of the grave as they found it; no discovery of haste, no sign of confusion, but all in order: the linen grave-clothes lying in one place, the napkin that was about his head not lying with them but folded together in a place by itself, indicating the perfect calmness and composure with which their Lord had risen—transported with no rapture or surprise, but, in this supreme moment, maintaining the same tranquility which had ever characterized him.

It is said they saw and believed, though as yet they did not under-stand the saying that he must rise from the dead; and they left the place and ran with the news to his disciples.

But Mary still lingers weeping by the empty tomb—type of too many of us, who forget that our loved ones have arisen. Through her tears she sees the pitying angels, who ask her, as they might often ask us, "Why do you weep?" She tells her sorrowful story—they have taken away her Lord and she knows not where they have laid him— and yet at this moment Jesus is standing by her, and one word from his voice changes all.

It is not general truth or general belief that our souls need in their anguish; it is one word from Christ to *us*, it is his voice calling us by name that makes the darkness light.

His voice calling us by name makes the darkness light.

Saturday in Easter Week

A reading from a sermon by Phillips Brooks on the resurrection.

One of the strange things in the whole history of Christianity has been the way in which many souls have seemed not merely to miss but to prefer to miss its great simplicity. What an amount of reverent and devoted study has been given to strange doctrines, such as the doctrine of the historic fall of man, or the doctrine of the second advent of the Savior, or the doctrine of the correspondence of the types of the Old Testament with the events of the New, or the doctrine of the imputed righteousness of Christ. Human minds have hovered around them with a strange, unhealthy fascination. Theories have risen from them like mists out of dim fields, often very beautiful, as beautiful as they were thin and unsubstantial; while all the time the great solid truths, of our divine lineage and God's much-manifested love and Christ's redemption of the soul by sacrifice have lain, not denied, but unopened, unsounded for the depths of unfound richness that is in them. I am sure that much of the character of a Christian's faith may be tested by its simplicity, by whether we find abundant richness in the great, primary fundamental truths or whether our minds wander among fantastic doctrines, and value ideas not for their naturalness but for their strangeness; not for the way in which they satisfy and feed, but for the way in which they startle and surprise the human soul.

There is no region in which all this is more true than in speculation about the life which lies beyond the grave. Nowhere does the difference between the healthiness of simplicity and the unhealthiness of complicated and elaborate curiosity so visibly appear. People who hardly believe that there is such a thing as a future life at all will speculate on its details, will sit holding their breath while mediums who have no touch of common sympathy try to bring souls together in carnal manifestation, whose intimacy is too sacred for any but themselves to share. It is not this that brings comfort and peace. It is not this that lifts the souls on earth to live already the divine life which their kindred souls are living in the celestial world. No morbid dream of knowledge which is not for me, no fancied sight into the detailed occupations of the spiritual life—only the great, broad, simple certainty that the friend I love is in the perfect company and care, is held fast in the tender and majestic love of God—only this I want to satisfy my soul. The Bible tells us one thing—only one—about the dead who have passed out of our sight. They are with God. How simple that is! How sufficient it becomes! How cheap and tawdry as we dwell in it, it makes the guesses and conceits with which people try to make real to themselves what the dead are doing! They are with God. Their occupations are ineffable. No tongue can tell their new, untasted joy. The scenery in the midst of which they live speaks to the spirit with voices which no words born of the senses can describe. But the companionship and care—those are the precious, those are the intelligible things. The dead are with God. O you who miss even today the sound of the familiar voices, the sight of the dear, familiar faces, believe and be more than satisfied with that.

A Christian's faith may be tested by its simplicity.

About the Authors

Lancelot Andrewes (1555–1626) served as bishop of Winchester and chair of the committee that produced the Authorized (King James) Version of the Bible. As a member of the first generation nurtured in an independent Church of England and nourished by the Book of Common Prayer, Andrewes was one of those who demonstrated with the holiness of their lives that the Anglican way could produce saints.

Thomas Becon (1513–1567) was educated at Cambridge and ordained a priest in 1533. By 1540, he had been arrested for preaching heresy and forced to recant. He lived in exile during the reign of Mary and then returned to become a canon of Canterbury Cathedral. His voluminous writings, which included a contribution to the Book of Homilies issued in the reign of Edward VI, were widely popular. He has been called "the most important and influential . . . of the devotional writers of the time."

Richard Meux Benson (1824–1915) was ordained in 1848 and made vicar of Cowley, a village near Oxford (though now a suburb). A sermon of John Keble persuaded him to found the first monastic order for men since the Reformation. Officially called the Society of St. John the Evangelist, the order is popularly known as the "Cowley Fathers" from the place where it was founded.

William Beveridge (1637–1708) was a student of Oriental languages and served as archdeacon of Colchester and prebendary of Canterbury Cathedral. He declined appointment as bishop of Bath and Wells in 1691, but became bishop of St. Asaph in Wales four years before his death.

Phillips Brooks (1813–1893) was rector of Trinity Church Boston for over twenty years before serving briefly as bishop of Massachusetts. Many volumes of his sermons were published and his hymn, "O little town of Bethlehem," is one of the best known of all Christmas hymns.

Myles Coverdale (1488–1568) was ordained priest in 1514 and became an early enthusiast for the reform movement gathering support throughout the country. Forced into exile, he took over the work of translating the Bible that William Tyndale had begun. The work was completed in 1539 and, by order of Thomas Cromwell, "set up in every parish church." Coverdale subsequently returned to England, was made bishop of Exeter, and remained a leader in the Puritan party for the rest of his life.

Thomas Cranmer (1489–1556) was appointed archbishop of Canterbury by Henry VIII in 1533. Although he was influenced by the reforms taking place in Europe under the inspiration of Martin Luther, John Calvin, and others, Cranmer is best known for publishing the first Book of Common Prayer in 1549. That book stressed the importance of baptism and the Scriptures in shaping the lives of Christians.

Morgan Dix (1827–1908) served as rector of Trinity Church Wall Street for forty-six years (1862–1908) and was assistant at the church for seven years before that. A graduate of the General Theological Seminary, Dix was ordained to the priesthood in 1853 and served as assistant at St. Mark's Church, Philadelphia, for two years before moving to Trinity, where he remained until his death.

John Donne (1571–1631) was an unsuccessful lawyer who was urged to seek ordination by the king and was made dean of St. Paul's Cathedral. Although he is better known today for his poetry, his sermons, prayers, and meditations are among the great monuments of the English language.

Mark Frank (1612–1664) was a scholar and preacher who served as master of Pembroke Hall and archdeacon of St. Alban's. He lost his position during the rule of Oliver Cromwell but was reinstated afterward.

Charles Gore (1853–1932) served successively as bishop of Worcester, Birmingham, and Oxford but it was through his writing that he worked to bring Catholic principles to bear on the social changes of the early twentieth century and the new trends in Old Testament studies.

George Herbert (1593–1632) was plagued by ill health throughout his short life, but graduated from Cambridge and held various offices there before being ordained a deacon about 1626 and married in 1628. He was appointed vicar of the parish of Bemerton about 1630 and wrote *A Priest to the Temple; or, The Country Parson*, describing his vision of the ministry. His poems were not published until after his death, but they have been recognized ever since as among the great poems in the English language.

Robert Herrick (1591–1674) is best remembered for the line "Gather ye rosebuds while ye may," but his poetry ranged from elegies and love songs to celebrations of rustic and ecclesiastical festivals. Ordained in 1623, he served as vicar of Dean Prior in Devonshire except during the Commonwealth.

John Keble (1792–1866) was a leader in the Tractarian Movement but was perhaps better known in his own day as the author of a collection of poems called *The Christian Year*. Although he served as professor of poetry at Oxford, the center of his ministry for the last thirty years of his life was as vicar of the parish of Hursley near Winchester.

Charles Kingsley (1819–1875) was ordained to the priesthood in 1842 and made Curate of Eversley, Hants, where he spent most of the rest of his life, although he served for a few years, simultaneously, as professor of modern history at Cambridge and also for brief periods as canon of Chester and Westminster Cathedrals. He became a leader in the Christian Socialist Movement and a critic of the Tractarian Movement, contributing essays to *Politics for the People* and *The Christian Socialist*. Among his novels, *Westward Ho!* may be the best known. He also wrote a popular children's book, *The Water-Babies*.

William Law (1686–1761) was one of those who refused to take the oath of loyalty to George I and therefore he was forced to live outside the established church. His *Serious Call to a Devout and Holy Life* nevertheless became one of the most widely read books of devotion ever published. He served as tutor to the father of Edward Gibbon and lived a life of great simplicity, working to organize schools and almshouses.

Hannah More (1745–1833), influenced by John Newton and a friend of Samuel Johnson, founded Sunday schools for children and wrote books on prayer and devotional subjects. For several years she produced three tracts a month with a tale, a ballad, and a tract for Sunday reading, which were sold for a penny.

John Newton (1725–1807) is best known today as the author of the hymn "Amazing Grace." He served as a ship's captain in the slave trade before his conversion and afterward as vicar of Olney, where he was an important influence in the Evangelical revival.

Francis E. Paget (1851–1911) served as vicar of Bromsgrove and then, at Oxford, as Regius professor of Pastoral Theology, dean of Christ Church, and finally bishop. He was a strong supporter of the Oxford Movement, contributing an essay on the sacraments to *Lux Mundi* and editing an edition of Hooker's *Ecclesiastical Polity*. His own developed spirituality is reflected in his *Spirit of Discipline*, published in 1891.

Edward Bouverie Pusey (1800–1882) was a principal leader of the Oxford Movement, contributing several of the tracts that were a feature of the effort to recover the Catholic heritage of the Church of England. He was appointed Regius professor of Hebrew at Oxford in 1828, the same year in which he was ordained, and held that position the rest of his life.

Frederick W. Robertson (1816–1853) was appointed to serve Trinity Chapel Brighton in 1846, and his preaching gained a very wide influence, especially with the working classes who were at that time largely untouched by the Church of England. His support of the revolutionary ideas circulating in 1848 stirred up controversy and hastened his early death.

Christina Rossetti (1830–1894) was the author of the familiar Christmas carol "In the bleak mid-winter" and a number of other books of poetry and theology, including a study of the book of Revelation.

Elizabeth Rowe (1674–1737) was encouraged to write by Bishop Thomas Ken of Bath and Wells and published several biblical character sketches. Her devotional prose was not published until after her death. The fervor of her language embarrassed her editor, who modified language that he considered too extravagant.

Henry Smith (c. 1550–1591) was "esteemed the miracle and wonder of his age" because of his remarkable memory and because of his eloquent and practical way of preaching.

Harriet Beecher Stowe (1811–1896) was the daughter, sister, and mother of prominent Congregational clergy but became a member of the Episcopal Church in Connecticut and worked with the bishop of Florida to build an Episcopal church near her winter home. Although she is chiefly known as the author of *Uncle Tom's Cabin*, she wrote several devotional books as well.

G. A. Studdert-Kennedy (1883–1929), who served as a chaplain in World War I, was one of the best-known preachers of his day and well known also for his poetry.

Jeremy Taylor (1613–1667) served as chaplain to King Charles I and chaplain to the Royalist army during the Civil War and then, during the Commonwealth, lived in retirement as chaplain to Lord Carberry's family in Wales. It was during this time that he wrote *Holy Living* and *Holy Dying*, his most influential books. After the restoration of the monarchy, Taylor was made bishop of Down and Connor in Ireland and served as vice-chancellor of Trinity College, Dublin.

William Temple (1881–1944) was bishop of Manchester (1921), archbishop of York (1929), and briefly archbishop of Canterbury (1942–1944). He was chair of the commission that produced an important study of doctrine in the Church of England and author of a number of important philosophical works as well as a study of St. John's gospel and a book on Christianity and the social order.

Thomas Traherne (1636–1674) grew up amid the turmoil of the English Civil War and turned his thoughts to God in the peaceful beauty of the English countryside. The works for which Traherne is now known were rediscovered in 1896 and, because they were unsigned, were only with difficulty identified as his work. The rapturous mysticism that they express has drawn attention to them in a modern world that has much in common with the insecure world of Traherne. In a war-torn world dominated by thoughts of human sin, Traherne's writings are concerned almost exclusively with the beauty of nature and the glory of God.

Christopher L. Webber (1932–) served as a parish priest in inner city and suburban parishes as well as in the English-language parish of the diocese of Tokyo before moving to two small rural parishes in the northwest corner of Connecticut. He has written a number of books on aspects of the Episcopal Church and hymns that are included in several U.S. and Canadian hymnals.

Rowan Williams (1950–) was professor of theology at Oxford from 1986 to 1992, and then became bishop of Monmouth in Wales. He was made archbishop of Wales in 2000 and of Canterbury in 2002. He has written a number of books on the history of theology and spirituality and published collections of articles and sermons, as well as two books of poetry

Bibliography

Andrewes, Lancelot. XXVI *Sermons by the Right Honorable and Reverend Father in God, Lancelot Andrewes.* London: George Miller, 1629.

Thomas Becon. *Early Works of Thomas Becon.* Edited by John Ayre. Cambridge: The Parker Society, University Press, 1843.

Richard Meux Benson. *Redemption: Some of the Aspects of the Work of Christ Considered in a Course of Sermons.* London: J. T. Hayes, 1861.

William Beveridge. "The Works of William Beveridge." Pages 583–98 in Paul Elmer More and Frank Leslie Cross, *Anglicanism.* New York: Macmillan, 1957.

Brooks, Phillips. *The Candle of the Lord and Other Sermons.* New York: E. P. Dutton, 1902.

———. *Sermons.* New York: E. P. Dutton, 1901.

———. *Phillips Brooks: Selected Sermons.* Edited by William Scarlett. New York: H. P. Dutton, 1950.

Coverdale, Myles. *Remains of Myles Coverdale: Bishop of Exeter.* Cambridge: The Parker Society, University Press, 1846.

———. *Writings and Translations of Myles Coverdale.* Edited by George Pearson. Cambridge: The Parker Society, University Press, 1844.

Cranmer, Thomas. *Prayer.* Vol. I of *Tracts of the Anglican Fathers.* London: William Edward Painter, n.d.

Morgan Dix. *Sermons Doctrinal and Practical.* New York: E. P. Dutton, 1878.

Donne, John. *John Donne: Selections from Divine Poems, Sermons, Devotions, and Prayers.* Edited by John Booty. Mahwah, NJ: Paulist Press, 1990.

————. *The Sermons of John Donne.* Vol. 2. Edited by George R. Potter and Evelyn Simpson. Berkeley: University of California Press, 1953–1962.

Ferris, Theodore Parker. *The Image of God.* New York: Oxford University Press, 1965.

Frank, Mark. *Sermons.* Vol. I. Oxford: John Henry Parker, 1849.

————. *Sermons.* Vol. II. Oxford: John Henry Parker, 1849.

Gore, Charles. *The Incarnation of the Son of God.* Bampton Lectures for 1891. New York: Charles Scribner's Sons, 1891.

Herbert, George. *The Works of George Herbert.* London: Oxford University Press, 1941.

Herrick, Robert. "True Lent." *The Poetical Works of Robert Herrick.* Edited by F. W. Moorman. New York: Oxford University Press, 1921.

John Keble. *Sermons for Easter to Ascension Day.* Oxford: James Parker & Co., 1876.

————. *Sermons for the Holy Week.* Oxford: James Parker & Co., 1876.

Kingsley, Charles. *The Good News of God: Sermons by Charles Kingsley.* Boston: E. P. Dutton, 1865.

————. "The Message of Christ to the Working Man." Pages 255–57 in *Sermons and Society.* Edited by Paul A. Welsby. London: Penguin Books, Cox & Wyman Ltd., 1970.

Law, William. "The Spirit of Prayer." Pages 148–49 in *The Pocket William Law.* London: Latimer House Ltd., 1950.

More, Hannah. *The Book of Private Devotion.* Hartford: Brown & Parsons, 1841.

————. *Reflections on Prayer.* Philadelphia: A. Finley, 1820.

Newton, John. *Messiah: His Character, Advent, and Humiliation.* Philadelphia: William Young, 1797.

Paget, Francis E. *Sermons on Duties of Daily Life.* Philadelphia: Thomas Wardle, 1844.

Pusey, Edward B. *Parochial Sermons.* Vol. II. Oxford: James Parker & Co., 1869.

Robertson, Frederick W. *Sermons Preached at Trinity Chapel, Brighton.* Boston: Ticknor & Fields, 1859.

Rossetti, Christina. *Time Flies: A Reading Diary.* London: SPCK, 1895.

Elizabeth Rowe. *Devout Exercises of the Heart, in Meditations and Soliloquy, Prayer and Praise: by the Late Pious and Ingenious Mrs. Elizabeth Rowe.* New York: Ezekiel Cooper & John Wilson, 1808.

Smith, Henry. *The Sermons of Mr. Henry Smith,* quoted in *Sermons and Society.* Edited by Paul A. Welsby. London: Penguin Books, Cox & Wyman Ltd., 1970.

Stowe, Harriet Beecher. *Earthly Care.* Boston: J. P. Jewett & Co., 1855.

———. *Footsteps of the Master.* New York: J. B. Ford & Co., 1877.

Studdert-Kennedy, G. A. *I Believe: Sermons on the Apostles' Creed.* New York: George A. Doran Co., 1921.

———. *The Wicket Gate.* New York: George H. Doran Co., 1923.

Taylor, Jeremy. *Select Sermons.* London: Joseph Rickerby, 1836.

Temple, William. *Christus Veritas,* London: Macmillan, 1954.

Traherne, Thomas. *Poems, Centuries, and Three Thanksgivings.* Edited by Anne Ridler. London: Oxford University Press, 1966.

Vogel, Arthur. *The Power of His Resurrection.* New York: Seabury, 1976.

Webber, Christopher L. "Fear Not." Page 45 in *Meditations on Matthew.* Cincinnati: Forward Movement Publications, 1989.

Williams, Rowan. *A Ray of Darkness.* Cambridge: Cowley Publications, 1995.

ALSO BY CHRISTOPHER L. WEBBER

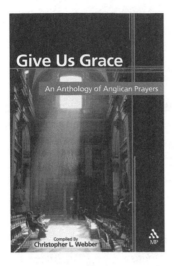

Give Us Grace
An Anthology of
Anglican Prayers

"Webber has done us an
indescribable favor in collecting
this vast treasure for our
devotional use."—*The Living
Church*

"In this useful and moving
anthology, old prayers can sound
modern while new ones bow to
the past. They remind us that, from the beginning, the word
was made prayer." —*Episcopal Life*

"*Give Us Grace* is a feast! This is a work of impressive
scholarship whose depths cannot be plumbed, yet at the
same time is remarkably accessible. It is not to be read but to
be savored. For anyone who loves the Anglican tradition of
prayer it will prove a faithful and reliable friend."
—Margaret Guenther, author of *Holy Listening*

◆ ◆ ◆

Morehouse books are available through bookstores,
from online booksellers, or directly from the publisher.
Call 800-877-0012 between 8:00 a.m. and 5:30 p.m.
(you may leave voice mail at other times) or
order online at www.morehousegroup.com.

Also by Christopher L. Webber

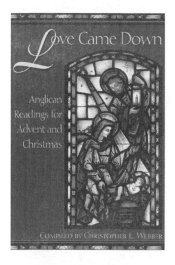

Love Came Down
Anglican Readings for
Advent and Christmas

"Webber's collection of Anglican
readings for Advent and the
12 days of Christmas is a feast
for the mind and the heart."
—*Publishers Weekly*

"There is more than inspiration
here, although there is that, and
there is more than a nice friendly
pat on the shoulder. Each reading has something for us to
think about and digest and then turn into flesh, muscle, and
deed." —*The Episcopal New Yorker*

"*Love Came Down: Anglican Readings for Advent and Christmas*
facilitates a daily quiet time for reflection during Advent, when
everything seems to accelerate. . . . Good reason to follow this
pilgrimage which is thoughtful and refreshing." —*Anglican
Journal*

◆ ◆ ◆

Morehouse books are available through bookstores,
from online booksellers, or directly from the publisher.
Call 800-877-0012 between 8:00 a.m. and 5:30 p.m.
(you may leave voice mail at other times) or
order online at www.morehousegroup.com.